Prayers for When You're Mad, Sad, or
Just Totally Confused

Prayers for When You're Mad, Sad, or Just Totally Confused

BRITTANY WAGGONER

VINE
BOOKS

SERVANT PUBLICATIONS
ANN ARBOR, MICHIGAN

Vine Books is an imprint of Servant Publications especially designed to serve evangelical Christians.

Servant Publications—Mission Statement
We are dedicated to publishing books that spread the gospel of Jesus Christ, help Christians to live in accordance with that gospel, promote renewal in the church, and bear witness to Christian unity.

The personal stories in this book are based on real events, although names and circumstances have been changed to protect the privacy of those involved.

Published by Servant Publications
P.O. Box 8617
Ann Arbor, Michigan 48107
www.servantpub.com

Cover design: PAZ Design Group, Salem, Oreg.

02 03 04 05 10 9 8 7 6 5 4 3 2

Printed in the United States of America
ISBN 1-56955-310-6

Dedication

To my loving grandmother,
Loretta Jean Pursley,
who believed in me without question.

Contents

Acknowledgments

To my Abba, whose friendship never ceases to amaze me. Thank you for the privilege to serve you.

To my parents, Reverend Jay and Dianne Waggoner. These are the lessons you have taught me. What you have given is invaluable.

Thank you to the gracious staff of Servant Publications for taking a chance on me. Thank you especially to Heidi Saxton, Shari MacDonald Strong, and Kathy Deering.

To my kindred spirits at CLASServices.com, thank you for letting me dream with you.

A special thank-you to Cedarville University, Fellowship Baptist Church, and the Voice of Faith Network in Apex, North Carolina.

Finally, to Dexter and Velma Daniels, Jim and Doris Layton, Ken Wales, Tim Beatty, Rachel Williams, Frank Saul, Joel Warder, Kim Hodge, David McClain, the Worstell family, Cheryl Davis, and Sam Smith, thank you for keeping a smile on my face and hope in my heart.

Introduction

The first time I can remember being disappointed, I was six years old. My dad had gone to the store to run some errands. He came back with a smile on his face and said, "Britt, I brought your favorite gum!" My hopes shot sky high and my eyes widened with anticipation. He pulled the small red package out of the stiff brown bag. I looked at the present in disbelief. Where was my Juicy Fruit? This imposter was most definitely not my favorite! I didn't even like this kind of gum! I knew my father loved me, but this was not what I had in mind.

In that moment I was disappointed. It probably wasn't the first time, and it definitely wasn't the last. No doubt, you've felt the sting of disappointment, too. Disappointment is universal to all ages, peoples, and geographic areas. Our disappointments can come in all shapes and sizes. We all hurt and we all wish the things that hurt us didn't happen. At times we are all mad, sad, or just totally confused.

Did you ever play freeze tag as a child? In this game players run around crazily until the player who is "It" tags them. Once tagged, the players become frozen in place. The game continues all around the frozen statues, but the people who have been tagged are left to pause for breath and gather their thoughts until another player rescues them and returns them to the game.

In real life, disappointment often "tags" us as well, bringing our lives to a screeching halt. When disappointment hits, we, too, become "frozen." When that happens, we have to make a

11

decision: How will we react? Are we out of the game for good? Or will we seize the opportunity to catch our breath and learn from our experience so that we can play the game even better once we are "unfrozen" and become active players again?

Our reaction depends on our perspective. The most important point in the story I shared a moment ago was not the kind of gum I wanted but the fact that my father loved me. When you find yourself frozen in a less-than-ideal situation, realize that the moment is not just a disappointment but also an *appointment* with opportunity. God wants to meet you in every moment. He wants to remind you that he loves you and is in total control of the circumstances of your life. Prayer is an opportunity to meet him in whatever heartache you are facing.

> *They go down again to the depths: their soul is melted because of trouble. They reel to and fro, and stagger like a drunken man, and are at their wit's end. Then they cry unto the Lord in their trouble, and he bringeth them out of their distresses. He maketh the storm a calm, so that the waves thereof are still ... he bringeth them into their desired haven.*
>
> PSALM 107:26b-30, KJV

Painful disappointments are found in every corner of life, and the feelings they trigger often linger in our hearts long after the original experiences are past. This reality is one of the hardest lessons you or I will ever learn. Yet God *is* here, and he is waiting for you. It is my hope that this truth will be made clear to you in these pages and that you will find comfort as you face your own disappointments. I hope, also, to encourage you to bring each disappointment to the God who loves you and who is with you, not only in the joyful but also in the most challenging times in your life.

How to Use This Book

This book is designed for the disappointed child of God. Each chapter addresses a different emotion or disappointment that you may be facing. The main text of the chapter is there to help you understand what you are feeling and how it can be faced with God's help. At the end of each chapter you will find Prayer Starters, a Scripture assignment, and a sample prayer.

The Prayer Starters are just what they sound like: these sections help you think about and deal with your own situation while prompting you to bring all that you are feeling to the throne of God. The Scripture assignment may be used during your quiet time, or you may use it as extra reading. Finally, the sample prayer is there to give you a skeleton prayer you can use and embellish upon to tell God what you are going through.

To get the most out of each chapter, you may want to highlight the statements you identify with most, keep a journal of the actual prayers that result from each chapter, or both. As you read this book remember that God's Word tells us in Hebrews 4:16, "Let us approach the throne of grace with confidence, so that we may receive mercy and find grace to help us in our time of need."

God bless,
Brittany Waggoner

ONE

When You Are Stressed Out

A few years ago when I was a high school senior, I began working on a television show for Christian teens called "Teen Scene." It was one of the most enjoyable times in my life! We had special segments on Christian colleges and Christian music, stories about local teens, and guest speakers such as youth pastors and teen counselors. While these varied elements added to the excitement and variety of the show, they also added to my stress.

In addition to being in my last year of high school, which was no piece of cake, I was fully involved at my church and I had to balance friends and family on top of my other responsibilities. I honestly did not think my busy lifestyle affected me that much. I suspected I was pretty stressed, but I also thought that was to be expected. After all, I did not have a chance to exercise, eat well, or sleep as much as I should have during that time. I wasn't putting nearly enough energy and time into my studies and relationships, but I was so busy that I barely noticed.

My overcommitment finally caught up with me, but not until my first year at college. I had been running non-stop and I did not slow down when I reached Cedarville. I was so excited to be at a Christian university filled with great people that I rarely slept more than five or six hours a night. I was always talking to someone in the dorm or on the phone.

Soon after my first quarter at school, I became very tired and noticed that my throat had become swollen. I went to the doctor and found out I had mono! Several girls from my hall had already been sick with mononucleosis. Most commonly experienced by people ages fifteen to twenty-four, this virus can cause fatigue, weakness, sore throat, fever, swollen tonsils, headache, loss of appetite, and a soft, swollen spleen. There is no specific cure for mono other than bed rest and adequate fluid intake. Maybe God knew that only a sickness that forced me to rest would slow me down.

Looking back now, it's not a surprise to me that I became ill. When we do not take good care of our bodies they cannot fight off sickness. Our bodies can take only so much stress before they need rest. If we don't recognize the need to slow down and take the appropriate action, our bodies will slow us down through sickness. Mono was not fun, but I most certainly learned a lesson. Now, as a sophomore in college, my favorite pastime is no longer staying up at night; it's sleeping all the time, anytime!

Of course, some types of stress can actually be positive. When I have a paper due and I have just two hours to write it, I generally rise to the occasion with more creativity than I would have had previously. This positive stress is what the stress books call "eustress." *The Complete Idiot's Guide to Managing Stress* defines it this way: "*eustress* ... is what gets you up and running, what enables you to get to work, get to the ball game on time, or clean out the garage on Saturday. Eustress helps to make your life enjoyable, even interesting. Such stress provides stimulation and challenges that are essential to development, growth, and change."[1] Athletes talk about how their nervous energy gives them extra adrenaline. This is an example of eustress.

Now, how do we tell the difference between bad and good stress? Stress is good only if it is short-lived. If the stress continues to the point of exhaustion it no longer has a positive effect on us. Again, *The Complete Idiot's Guide to Managing Stress* warns: "Bad stress, or *distress,* makes you anxious and irritable, dampens your spirits, and shortens your life. Distress is a reaction to some type of pressure, either external or self-imposed, which prompts psychological and physiological changes of an undesirable nature." [2] The point of this chapter is to identify what causes us bad or prolonged stress, so that we can disarm its negative effects.

Seek the Source

When we visit the doctor because we are sick the first thing he or she asks is, "Where does it hurt?" The doctor must identify the source of our discomfort. We need to do the same when we are trying to "diagnose" our stresses. Before we can tackle our stress we need to know exactly where it is coming from. For example, the stress that comes from a dating relationship is very different from the stress of an unemployed father. Each will need to be dealt with differently.

To seek the source of your stress, sit down in a relaxing spot at a time when you are not under a time crunch and list everything that currently worries you, stresses you, or makes you unhappy. You might jot down some reasons why each of these things is stressful. Sometimes this process helps us realize that our problems aren't as big as they seem. At other times, it reveals to us that we are not outwardly acknowledging all that we are really feeling and experiencing.

Once you have made your list, cross out all of the items about which there is no point in worrying. You must decide which items on your list are *worth* stressing over.

If you are stressed because your bedroom isn't clean, you may realize that worrying about it isn't worth the emotional toll it takes and simply decide to clean it when you can. Scratch it off the list! However, if a messy room is causing major relationship problems between you and your mom, it is something you need to deal with soon. The purpose of good stress is to motivate us to make positive changes in our lives.

Highlight the items on your list that deserve your focus. After identifying the causes of stress in your life you'll be much better prepared to take action and deal with them.

Turn to Others

Scripture says, "Two are better than one, because they have a good return for their work: If one falls down, his friend can help him up" (Eccl 4:9-10a). This is important to remember, because when stress hits, we can easily be tempted to deal with everything by ourselves.

After I began working on "Teen Scene," I became so used to being stressed that whenever some new problem or issue came up I tried to deal with it on my own. My parents used to joke that I was addicted to stress, because I would pile up responsibilities on myself and rarely ask for help. In the beginning, I would try to write the shows and book the guests on my own, which is a lot more work than it sounds. As much as I disliked asking for help, though, I eventually came to a point where I had no choice.

My parents became my biggest source of help and comfort. My mother, who is a writer as well, started to help me write the shows. My father came up with ideas for show topics and also worked on the sets. It is amazing how much can be done with the help of others! Eventually I was able to build a small staff for the show. I was then able to delegate last-minute tasks and focus on the big picture. The result was a better-quality show, because everyone was able to focus on his or her own job.

Of course, sometimes turning to others is not about delegating tasks but about seeking emotional and spiritual support. Just today, I was worried about trying out for a school play, so I asked a friend of mine in passing to remember me in prayer. It does not take a lot of effort on our part to seek support in stressful times. We shouldn't be afraid to ask someone to pray for us, either. Prayers are like breath mints: you can never have enough!

It is also beneficial to talk about your stress with a close friend or relative. Oftentimes, when we talk about our problems we find that they aren't as earth shattering as they seemed in our minds.

Rely on God

Other people can help relieve some stress in our lives, but we sometimes forget that God can do much more for us than anyone else can. He is our Rock, our constant source of love and encouragement. He will listen and not grow tired. He will constantly sustain us. The single most important thing to remember when we are under stress is to pray. The apostle Paul writes: "Do not be anxious about anything, but in everything, by prayer and petition, with thanksgiving, present your requests to God. And the peace of God, which transcends all understanding, will guard your hearts and your minds in Christ Jesus" (Phil 4:6-7). Notice that after you present your requests to God in prayer with thanksgiving the peace will come.

In high school I did a lot of baby-sitting to earn extra cash. One of the little girls I baby-sat was a very compassionate little girl named Sophia. What I remember most about Sophia was her habit of rescuing every bug that managed to get into the house. Whenever she spotted one she wanted me to catch it in a jar and release it outside. I once thought that she was playing in another room when I tried to kill a spider. She wasn't. Sophia came sprinting to my side, begging for the life of that spider. After I got the nasty little thing into a jar, she took it from me and gently carried it to the front lawn. She didn't even force it out of the jar. She waited patiently until the spider was ready to brave the jungle of the lawn.

This is a picture of what God does for us in stressful times. David speaks to God in Psalm 32:7, saying, "You are my hiding place; you will protect me from trouble." If we allow him, God will surround us with his loving hands and give us a hiding place until we are strong enough to face the world again.

It's Time to Get Physical

Our bodies need certain things to function properly (such as food, water, and air), and our minds and emotions need our bodies to be healthy before *they* can function properly. If you are not eating well, sleeping enough, or exercising enough, your unhealthy lifestyle could be affecting your emotions.

There is a definite connection between the amount of stress we feel and how much exercise we are getting. *The Complete Stress Management Workbook* makes this point: "An effective exercise program can reduce your brain stress and body stress, improve health, firm muscles, and help you lose weight."[3]

Sleep is a major issue for teens and young adults. We either get too much or, more commonly, not enough. According to an article by Jason Cohen, CBS Health Watch teen correspondent, when fifty students were asked which health factor—food, sleep, alcohol, or drugs—had the biggest effect on them in college, the most common answer was sleep (or the lack thereof).[4] If you are getting too little sleep, realize that this must become a priority. Getting it—or not getting it—will affect your attitude, your health, and your whole day.

Nutrition can affect us in the same ways. Although it is tempting to live off of Mountain Dew and pizza, your body needs a more balanced diet than that. Even though your physical habits are probably not the primary reason for your stress level, they are a contributing factor worth examining.

Dealing with stress is a full-time job for your body. Without the physical support of enough sleep, energy gained from exercise, and vitamins obtained through a balanced diet, stress can become a serious problem.

Be a Good Steward

Growing up in a Christian home and attending a Christian school, I was taught from a young age to be a good steward. I would often hear pastors and teachers speak of being a good steward with money, talents, and time. It wasn't until I had finished my first year of college that I realized that I needed to be a good steward of my energy as well.

One of my greatest struggles was getting involved in too many clubs, committees, and social events. I would wear myself out and then find that I had no time for my schoolwork. On a typical day I would go to classes, attend a meeting for my campus organization, brainstorm with a group of people from my church ministry, answer email for an hour, and go out to dinner with friends. After dinner I had other meetings to attend. By the time I had gotten everything accomplished for the day, it was ten o'clock!

It is easy for us to think that we are pleasing God by getting involved in every ministry that comes along. Yet I suspect that if we are putting only a little bit of energy into each one, God would rather we focused on a few. I had to limit my involvement in order to maintain a happy and healthy lifestyle.

You and I are our own most precious resources. Some stress is self-inflicted; we bite off more than we can chew and then get stressed out. Being a good steward of self requires that we learn how much we can handle and say no to what we cannot.

Stop Worrying, Start Relaxing

Stress and worry are siblings. Worry causes stress; sometimes stress causes more worry. They are inseparably linked. In *God, I've Got a Problem,* Ben Ferguson explains worry: "In the New Testament, 'worry' (*merimna*) comes from the Greek verb *merizo* which means 'to divide.' People who worry are 'divided'— mentally torn apart."[5]

Worry does tear us apart. Some people by nature worry more than others. When my mother doesn't have something to worry about she will worry that she is missing something and worry anyway! Piling up more and more worries about things that *could* happen is like loading up a van that doesn't have tires. The worries aren't going anywhere; they are just sitting there.

Jesus spoke about worry in Matthew 6:26-27, saying, "Look at the birds of the air; they do not sow or reap or store away in barns, and yet your heavenly Father feeds them. Are you not much more valuable than they? Who of you by worrying can add a single hour to his life?"

Jesus defines worry as a lack of trust in God. Placing our burdens on him is the only thing that can release us from our worry. "Casting the whole of your care—all your anxieties, all your worries, all your concerns, once and for all—on Him; for He cares for you affectionately and cares about you watchfully" (1 Pt 5:7, AMP).

When we do lay our problems at God's feet we can finally sit back and relax. Unfortunately, we often have the wrong perspective. We think that at the end of the day, when we tell God all our problems, we can climb into a comfy chair and relax. I think "casting our cares" should be more like a comfortable coat that we wear everywhere we go. Relaxing into God's loving care can be something we do all day long.

Stress is a part of life. There will be times of little stress and times when you have nothing *but* stress! However, no matter how much stress you have, God remains the same. He is consistently bigger than any of your problems or worries. Unlike you and me, he is thoroughly stress-free and waiting to give us peace in the midst of our chaos.

Prayer Starters

What is causing you stress? _____

_____

_____

How do you commonly deal with stress?

_____

_____

What's the one thing you'd like to change about the stress in your life? _____

_____

_____

Scripture Assignment

Matthew 6:24-31

A Prayer for When You Are Stressed Out

Sovereign God,

I am so busy and so stressed out that I cannot seem to find any relief except when I'm with you. It just seems like I cannot keep everyone happy without making myself unhappy. Give me the strength to say no to the activities and ministries that I don't have time for. Help me to focus my energy on the work you have given me and not be distracted by anything else.

Help me to take care of my physical body so that when these times of stress hit I will be able to stand strong. God, please help me to cast all my cares on you all day long and not worry about the future. Thank you for being in control of all that I am not.

In your name,

Amen

TWO

When You Are Struggling
With Your Self-Image

I love to teach, and most Sunday mornings you can find me in a classroom, teaching children. One of my favorite former students from a weekly Bible Club is a girl named Casey. She had a very sweet spirit and a desire to know God. I enjoyed making eye contact with her during the Bible story because I knew she was excited to learn about him.

However, although Casey was amazing in my eyes, she did not see herself that way. Casey rode to Bible Club every week with her neighbor, Abby. It was very hard for Casey to be friends with Abby because Abby's parents bought her anything she wanted. Abby always had the best jewelry, makeup, and clothing. Casey did not have money for new clothes or shoes.

Every Sunday I would watch those two girls sitting next to one another: Abby giggling and showing off and Casey quietly taking it all in. I looked into her eyes and saw her spirit crying. Because she didn't have the best clothes or the coolest friends, Casey felt like she wasn't as special as the other girls. The way she viewed herself affected her schoolwork and her relationships with those around her. The way she felt on the inside affected her outside world. I still pray that one day she will see exactly how special she is.

The truth is, when we feel bad about ourselves we feel bad about everything. In *Our Unmet Needs*, Charles Stanley describes the pain of low self-esteem: "When a person does not have a healthy sense of self-worth, he will always have an inner feeling of something lacking. He will have an abiding feeling of need-iness, of feeling on the outside, of feeling like an observer, of feeling hungry and dissatisfied for something more in life."[1]

Have you ever felt as though you were lacking something important, something you really needed? A lot of people feel this way. We think we have to have a particular relationship, job, or achievement to be valuable.

At my high school, all the "popular" girls had boyfriends. If you didn't have one then something had to be wrong with you—at least that's how I felt. I was without a boyfriend for the majority of high school, but that didn't mean that I wasn't worth as much as the other girls. Sometimes it was hard to look around and see all the happy couples. I had to fight the temptation to believe I was less of a person because I didn't have a boyfriend.

It is dangerous to allow other people's opinions of us to change our opinions of ourselves. No matter what any person thinks of us, the Scriptures reflect an accurate picture of how valuable we are.

We Are Fearfully and Wonderfully Made

When I was in the third grade, my family moved from West Virginia to North Carolina. Some of the kids in my new school thought it was fun to tease all of the new students. It wasn't long before they were making jokes about me in front of the whole class. At first they made fun of me being from West

Virginia. Then one student decided to look up my name in the dictionary. He found "Brittany spaniel," which is a type of hunting dog. All of the West Virginia jokes turned into dog jokes. It may sound ridiculous now, but it was traumatic for an eight-year-old. Often I came home from school feeling bad about myself.

One day, my mom showed me the following passage from the Book of Psalms. It really helped me to realize who I am to God. Ever since that incident, when I have felt down about myself I have read it again.

> O Lord, you have searched me and you know me. You know when I sit and when I rise; you perceive my thoughts from afar.... For you created my inmost being; you knit me together in my mother's womb. I praise you because I am fearfully and wonderfully made; your works are wonderful, I know that full well.... All the days ordained for me were written in your book before one of them came to be.
>
> PSALM 139:1-2, 13, 16

God saw us and was with us before we were even born. The world often tells us that at that stage in life we were only fetuses, but God says that he cared for us even in our mothers' wombs. We have all been created in amazing ways we cannot comprehend or describe. You and I are living masterpieces, designed by God himself.

Andrea Stephens speaks of our unique creation in her book, *God Thinks You're Positively Awesome!*

The way you are designed reveals another aspect of God's creativity. You are complete and perfect in his eyes. You and I are God's work of art! We each have his signature touch. We are different from each other. Yet we are both valuable creations, molded and decorated by the Master Designer. And we are equally attractive to our Father God.[2]

Has a small child ever come up to you and shown you a picture he or she has drawn? Undoubtedly, the child was thrilled to present such a precious masterpiece. It would be positively horrible to declare such a picture ugly. The child would be crushed!

Surely God wants us to appreciate his true masterpieces. God's artwork is his creation, and you and I are part of that intricate design. We are among his best and favorite works of art.

Loving Others As We Love Ourselves

Do you remember having to split something with someone else when you were a child? Maybe you had to share a Snickers bar. Undoubtedly, when the splitting was done one half turned out to be bigger than the other. It was at that point that most of us either took the bigger half for ourselves or bit the "extra" off to make it even.

It may seem that such actions are based on too much self-love. However, they are often the result of too little self-esteem. If we view ourselves as lacking something that we need, we will be selfish rather than giving toward others. Jesus said in Mark

12:31, "love your neighbor as yourself." When he said "as your-self," he was not approving selfish behavior but making a comparison. Our love for others should be a reflection of how we love and care for ourselves. Low self-esteem leads to selfishness, which interferes with the expression of love.

One of my favorite movies is *While You Were Sleeping*. In the movie, Sandra Bullock's character is mistaken for a man's fiancée. To make things more confusing, the man is in a coma. In one hilarious scene she goes over to the man's apartment to feed his cat and explores his apartment for the first time. She finds that he has pictures of himself everywhere. When she opens his wallet, she finds that he has pictures of himself inside. As the movie unfolds you realize that this guy is completely self-centered and arrogant.

This is *not* an example of healthy self-love; more likely, it portrays overcompensation that comes from a poor self-concept. Most of us know that singing our own praises is not good, but neither is being unaware of how special we are. A healthy self-concept is the key to a healthy self-love that sets the standard by which we love others. Keeping this all in balance is tricky, and we should constantly be committed to prayer.

Christ Loved Us Enough to Pay the Ultimate Price

Jessica was salutatorian of her graduating class. Although she had the academic ability, it became clear that she would not be able to attend college, for financial reasons. Her parents both worked but the family never seemed to get ahead. Her father was employed at a computer factory, but was struggling to make a living due to the recent onset of multiple sclerosis. It looked like Jessica's dream of attending college would be crushed, though she hoped that one day it still might come true.

Jessica's father loved her so much he decided that he would do whatever it took to send her to college. He began working an extra shift at the factory *and* working as a part-time janitor for a local church on the weekends. He did this for six months but realized that it wasn't going to be enough. He stopped taking lunch breaks so he could work through lunch for a few extra dollars and save the money lunch would cost.

Throughout Jessica's last year of high school her father simply did not rest—even though his symptoms worsened. He worked through each shift without sleep or food. His body weakened and began to slow down. Though Jessica did not realize it, on her graduation day her father could barely get out of bed. That day, Jessica and her whole family arrived at the auditorium where the graduation was to be held. At her husband's request, Jessica's mother quickly exited the vehicle with Jessica's three brothers and went inside. Jessica began to get out herself, but her father stopped her.

"Sweetie, can we talk for just a second?"

"Dad, we really don't have time for one of your lectures ... now come on, let's get this over."

"Jessica. You are going to college." Her father tried to get her attention.

"Yeah, Dad, I know ... one of these days."

"No, Jessie. This fall."

Jessica's eyes widened and her mouth could not close. "But how, Dad?"

"I worked some more hours at work. I did it because of how valuable you are to me."

Tears began to swell in Jessie's eyes. "Dad, your M.S., you

can't work extra. That could mean ..."

"Never mind what it means. You are going to college. Now get in there and give a brilliant speech."

Jessica did give a brilliant speech, one she came up with on the spot, about how much her family, especially her father, meant to her. She spoke about dreams and about *fulfilled* dreams. Her father smiled and his heart was filled with joy.

We are all like Jessie. Our Father gave up everything for us when Christ died for us. He did so because of our value to him. The same God that we pray to every night is the Father who gave up everything so that we could be with him one day in heaven.

We are special because of the love that God has for us. And that is reason enough.

Prayer Starters

How do you feel about yourself?

_____

_____

_____

In what ways do you feel inadequate or inferior?

_____

_____

_____

Can you identify why you feel the way you do?

_____

_____

_____

Do you think it is possible that God made a mistake when he created you?

_____

_____

_____

How do you feel when you think of Christ's sacrifice for you?

_____

_____

Scripture Assignment
Exodus 3:11-12; 4:10-12

A Prayer for When You Are Struggling With Your Self-Image

Dear gracious Father,

I throw myself at your feet as I realize that I am nothing, but I lift my hands to you as I realize your love makes me more valuable than I can grasp. It is easy for me to take my eyes off of you and compare myself with those around me. I know this only causes me to feel inadequate and jealous. Help me keep my eyes toward heaven as I look forward to a day when I will be complete in you.

In your holy name,

Amen

THREE

When You Are Afraid

During my senior year of high school I began to do volunteer work at a Christian television station in Apex, North Carolina. I answered the phones, took out the trash, and ran errands for the receptionist. It was at this station that God allowed me to work on "Teen Scene."

One winter evening I asked the station director's wife if they had ever considered doing a show for teens. She mentioned that they had wanted to do a show like that for a long time but had never had anyone to host and produce it. I quickly told her that I would love to do something like that. She thought about it for a second and said, "I will make the appointment." She promptly made arrangements for me to meet with the executive producer and founder of the station, and instructed me to go home and brainstorm ideas.

When the day of the appointment came I was so excited I could barely stand it! The meeting was short and sweet. The producer asked me about my vision for the show, then said, "You had better get started. This show airs in three weeks." I couldn't believe it! I was excited but overwhelmed. My parents and I had the most stressful three weeks of our lives. We had to design and construct a set, book guests, recruit sponsors, and prepare a topic for discussion on the show. All of these things had to be done while I was attending school, teaching children's classes at church, leading a puppet team for my church, and doing what felt like a million other things related to family, friends, and schoolwork.

In all the rush and stress, I didn't have time to think about whether I could pull it off. Then one night it hit me as we were driving home after running some errands. As we drove over a small bridge I felt this huge weight in my stomach. All at once I began to doubt whether I could host a show. I had never hosted a show by myself. I was seventeen years old! What if it flopped? What if it was so bad they canceled it? What if I couldn't get guests every week? All those details were up to me as host and producer, and I was scared to death.

My fear was engulfing me, and the only thing I felt I could do was pray. After spending some time with God I decided that he had given me this opportunity for a purpose and that I needed to face my fear and trust him. The show, called "Teen Scene," was a success. God was gracious in allowing me to work on the show for two years. (However, to this day, I dislike crossing that bridge.)

When we are trusting in ourselves, we have every right to be fearful. We *should* be afraid! We are humans: capable of all kinds of catastrophes and mishaps. But when we trust instead in God's ability and ask him for help, we have absolutely nothing to fear.

The Mechanics of Fear

Kent Crockett defines fear in *The 911 Handbook* this way: "Fear is **F**alse **E**vidence **A**ppearing **R**eal. Most fears are our imaginations out of control. Because fear involves torment

(1 Jn 4:18), it will rob us of our peace and joy. It can also force us to make wrong decisions which keep us from reaching our full potential."[1]

Fear is, indeed, crippling. As with any other problem, we can allow it to control our lives or we can learn to control it. However, before we can deal with our fear we must identify it.

When I was very young, I used to have horrible nightmares about someone breaking into our home. I would wake up in the middle of the night so scared that I could not move. Frozen in my fear, it would take me a long time to muster the courage to grab my Bible. I would open it up to Psalm 139, where God speaks of being with us no matter where we are. I would read those verses over and over again until I could go back to sleep. Many mornings as a child, I would wake up clutching my Bible.

The story of my nightmare illustrates how we can best deal with our fears. When I woke up from the nightmare, I identified my fear that someone could be in the house. Next, I thought logically about my fear: If someone were in the house, my dog would have barked and my parents probably would have heard the intruder. I had to extract reality from my fear. Identifying and thinking logically about my fear helped, but the emotion of fear was still present. It was then that I reached for my Bible and was reminded of God's presence in my life. I prayed that God would calm my spirit so that I could relax and go back to sleep. "What time I am afraid, I will trust in thee" (Ps 56:3, KJV).

Although fears come in all shapes and sizes, the way we deal with them is with faith. It does not matter if you are afraid of heights, death, the future, rejection, failure, public speaking, or loneliness. All our fears can be conquered through prayer and trust in God. The word "prayer" evokes a vision of someone down on his or her knees in a prayer closet deeply pondering each request. Although this type of prayer is very beneficial and pleasing to God, our fears sometimes hit us at inconvenient times. Sometimes our prayers are whispered under our breath in a large crowd or are just thought in passing. There is nothing wrong with asking for God's help in this manner. The idea is reflected in 1 Thessalonians 5:17, which simply tells us to, "Pray without ceasing" (KJV).

The Opposite of Fear

After God's chosen people, the Israelites, had spent years of bondage in Egypt, Moses and Aaron led them into the wilderness in search of the Promised Land. Following decades of hardship, the time had come. Each of Israel's tribes sent one spy to sneak into the land to see who, if anyone, inhabited the land. They soon found that the land most certainly was inhabited, and by giants!

All but two of the spies reported that Israel should pack it in and give up. Most of these spies had their spiritual binoculars focused on the giants, but two of them had their lenses fixed on God. According to the story in Numbers 13 and 14, Caleb and Joshua were the only two spies who returned with hope of a victory over the giants.

Caleb and Joshua represented courage. They addressed the Israelites in Numbers 14:9, saying, "Only rebel not ye against the Lord, neither fear ye the people of the land; for they are bread for us: their defense is departed from them, and the Lord is with us: fear them not" (KJV).

The other spies continued to let their fear of the giants keep them from obeying God's command to take the land. Later in the chapter, God tells his people that those who do not believe will never see the Promised Land, but because of their faith, Caleb and Joshua will. "But my servant Caleb, because he had another spirit with him, and hath followed me fully, him will I bring into the land where into he went; and his seed shall possess it" (Nm 14:24, KJV).

It is interesting that the Lord described Caleb as having "another spirit." Caleb possessed the opposite of the spirit of fear. He had the spirit of faith.

You and I can develop our faith by continually relying on God through prayer. I remember times in my life when I prayed specific prayers that God answered in front of my eyes. Experiences like answered prayers build our faith and trust in God, but even unanswered prayers have helped me trust God more completely.

Have you ever watched "The Crocodile Hunter"? In that show, Australian Steve Irwin travels to different parts of the world to wrestle with some pretty scary creatures. I can usually handle watching it, but when he starts picking up snakes, I completely lose it. It doesn't matter the size, shape, or deadliness of the snake; I can barely watch it.

Fear is like one of those snakes. It can be a massive fear of death or of rejection, or it can be a small worry about a test grade. No matter what the size or shape, it is still fear and needs to be dealt with in the same way.

The apostle Paul tells his young friend Timothy in 2 Timothy

1:7 that, "God hath not given us a spirit of fear, but of power, and of love, and of a sound mind" (KJV). You and I have the "power" to identify and face our fear head-on. We have a "sound mind" to look rationally at our fear. "Love" should help us to fulfill our obligations, no matter what fear we are facing.

The Reality of Fear

Even though I was afraid to host "Teen Scene," I still had a responsibility to the TV station to do it. Sometimes we think that our fear gives us an excuse to leave our responsibilities and run for the hills. Fears that go unchecked can have some harsh results. Fear can keep us from relationships, keep us from going away to college, or keep us from serving God.

Think of the disastrous results that would have occurred if certain heroes of the Bible had let their fear keep them from their callings. What if Esther had been too afraid of King Xerxes' wrath to go before him and save her people? What if Noah had been too afraid of being ridiculed to build a boat? What if David had been too afraid of death to fight Goliath? Those people were all afraid, but they knew that no matter how they felt, they still had to follow God. Their emotions did not excuse them from achieving their purpose. Thank goodness that with God's help through prayer, we, too, can conquer fear and further his kingdom.

No Fear of the Future

My friends and I love playing GoldenEye on Nintendo 64. This James Bond game can be played by up to four people. You can pick the location, the weapons, and the characters you want. The object of the game is to find and attack the other players. I am not an amazing player, but I hold my own. I usually play against my best friends, Kim and Tim. When I started playing the game I could not win at all. I always seemed to lose. In the middle of one game, I threw down the controller in aggravation and decided to just watch Kim and Tim play. Then I noticed something. When they played, they immediately grabbed the nearest gun and started hunting other players. Both of them usually ended up with the best guns and the prime spots because they trusted that eventually those things would be there. I had been doing it all wrong! Whenever I started, I tried to find the best gun, get plenty of ammo and a prime location, and *then* start hunting the other players. I was afraid that if all of these key elements were not in place, I would lose. Yet in my quest to find all of these things I never noticed when someone was sneaking up on me.

The same thing is true in life. The best move isn't always to be scrambling for the best of everything. Instead, we need to live our lives today without fear of tomorrow. We can trust God for the things we need and start playing the game of life with wisdom and confidence.

Prayer Starters

What fears are keeping you from living the way you want to live? _____

_____

_____

_____

How are your fears affecting you spiritually, emotionally, and physically?

_____

_____

_____

What can you do about your fears?

_____

_____

_____

What have you learned about God through your fears?

_____

_____

_____

_____

Scripture Assignment
Joshua 1:5-9; Psalm 23:4; Isaiah 41:10

A Prayer for When You Are Afraid

Dear all-caring Father,

I know that in your Word you promise never to leave or forsake me (see Hebrews 13:5). I am so thankful that nothing can separate us. Your presence is comforting in my time of fear. Recently I have been very fearful about _____. Please help me to face my fear with your strength. I ask for a "peace that passes all understanding." Only you can bring me through this. Thank you for developing faith in my life.

In your Son's name,

Amen

FOUR

When Everything Goes Wrong

In the fall of my senior year, I was given a solo to sing in my high school choir. At the time, I felt like it was the only good thing happening in my life. My grandfather had passed away late that summer and I still was grieving over him. My best friend, Brett, had not come by to see me all summer. I attended a Christian high school and had what I thought were many solid Christian friendships, yet only two of my classmates had written or called me when my grandfather died. I felt so alone. I had lost my best friend, my grandfather, and it seemed most of my other friendships at school, all in just a few months.

The first week of practice on the solo, I sang my heart out. I allowed it to become the most important thing in my life because I felt that it was all that I had. The second week of practice, the director informed me that Anna, the other first soprano in the group, would be singing with me on the last line of the solo. I wondered why, but I was still happy that I had the majority of the solo. Anna was very talented. She competed in solo competitions every year and usually came back with a blue ribbon. Anna also had a boyfriend, was the homecoming queen, and always received straight "A's." Her life was together.

The third week of practice, our director told us that we would be performing for a Christian television station nearby and that my song would be performed. That day, I was particularly excited about practicing my solo since I knew that I would be performing on TV! Before we got started, the director gave me a sad look and said, in front of the entire class, "Brittany, I think we had better let Anna take your solo this time, since she has a stronger voice for this type of song. We want our lineup to be perfect for this concert. Maybe you can help Anna on that last high note, though." As if one last high note would console me on the loss of an entire solo! Our director could have at least told me in private that Anna was taking my solo. Instead, I was humiliated in front of the whole ensemble. I know that our director wanted only what was best for the group, but I don't think she understood how that decision hurt me.

On the night of the concert, everyone was excited. Before I knew it, we were in the middle of the concert and Anna's solo was next. As Anna beautifully sang my solo I felt convicted about my anger and bitterness. I asked the Lord for the strength to take a backseat gracefully.

After the concert was over, I began to explore the TV station. I was enthralled with Christian broadcasting. That very night, I approached the station's receptionist and asked about the possibility of working as an intern. The next week I was operating the cameras and answering the telephone.

The Lord opened door after door for me at that television station. Because of my work there, I was able to host and produce "Teen Scene." This, in turn, led to opportunities to speak to youth groups and eventually the opportunity to write this book. The disappointment of my lost solo was the snowflake that started an avalanche of blessings the Lord had planned for me. My disappointment turned into an appointment.

Sometimes disappointments don't come in neatly wrapped boxes labeled "bad breakup," "failed exam," or "fight with your brother." Sometimes life's UPS drops off so many boxes we don't know which one to open first. There will be times in our lives when everything goes wrong. I think of my high school friend, Jeremiah, whose longtime girlfriend broke up with him the day after he received news that his father was being unfaithful to his mother. I also think of my friend Elisabeth, who lost her mother to cancer in her senior year of high school and now may not have the money she needs for college.

At times, overcoming disappointments feels like climbing out of quicksand. Yet even in times of despair there is hope. Here is part of a prayer uttered by the psalmist after he'd been hit by a truckload of disappointments: "Why are you in despair, O my soul? And why have you become disturbed within me? Hope in God" (Ps 42:5, NASB). Evidently, the psalmist was exiled from his homeland. He was possibly a captive and daily had to endure the taunts of his enemies. Notice that he tells God exactly how he is feeling, and in his heart he is given the answer: "Hope in God." He had to believe that God loved him and was in control of all that was happening to him.

The Big Question

It is a human response to ask "Why?" when bad things happen. If you have ever spent any time baby-sitting, you know that no matter what you tell the children to do, they always ask, "Why?" We may not be children, but our response is the same when we are disappointed. Our response is even more emphatic when we face devastating disappointments or several disappointments at the same time.

The book of James gives us some insight into the question, "Why?" James says, "Consider it all joy, my brethren, when you encounter various trials, knowing that the testing of your faith produces endurance. And let endurance have its perfect result, that you may be perfect and complete, lacking in nothing" (Jas 1:2-4, NASB). Notice, we are to "consider" these trials to be a "joy." Say what? I don't know about you, but the trials I go through are not a party! This is precisely why the Scripture doesn't say, "it will be joyful to go through trials." Instead, it says that we should "consider," or look upon, our trials as a good thing. The key is our attitude, not the circumstances. That is the one thing we can change.

What is the key to changing our attitude? It is the assurance of what trials produce in our life. The process is not joyful, but the outcome is worth rejoicing over. Notice also the phrase, "encounter various trials." We all are bound to go through many different kinds of trials, not just one disappointment. This is the process God is using to produce something of value—endurance—in our lives.

Last fall, I decided to go running with my roommate, Rachel. I knew that she was an athlete but figured that I could keep up. Little did I know that Rachel had been on the track team in high school and had been running three miles every day during the summer. Needless to say, I couldn't keep up with her. Why? Because I did not have the endurance that she had.

Endurance is not only important to our physical bodies; enduring hard times in life is the key to developing spiritual maturity. God does not want us to remain baby Christians forever. There are many Christians who don't want to grow up spiritually, but we need to grow up. God wants us to mature into adult Christians who can take on more responsibility in his kingdom.

Do you remember how you felt before you learned to drive? You were not old enough yet but you wanted the responsibility. You studied for it and even dreamed about it. You wanted the authorities to recognize that you had the skill and maturity needed to operate a vehicle, and you were willing to do whatever it took to get your license. God wants us to long and strive for spiritual maturity in the same way. Spiritual maturity should be our goal, and we should be willing to endure whatever it takes to achieve it.

Bring on the Lemonade

One of Erma Bombeck's most widely known sayings is, "When life gives you lemons, make lemonade." Of course, we all know that is easier said than done. Yet the focus of that saying is our response to a problem. Life will undoubtedly give us lemons, but what we choose to do with those lemons is up to us.

Do you remember my friend Elisabeth, who lost her mother to cancer? Not only did she have to deal with the death of her mother; soon after her mother died she found out that her father had been cheating on her mother. She was crushed by the pain that surrounded her. As if all of that wasn't enough, less than a year later her father became engaged to a different woman. Once the two were married, this woman's children took over Elisabeth's house and even Elisabeth's room! Then her father decided to remodel the house to accommodate his new bride and family, using much of Elisabeth's college fund. When I heard her story, I was amazed at how Elisabeth dealt with all of these circumstances. Every means of support that she had was ripped away from her. She lost her mother, her home, her college fund, and, in a sense, her father. The only thing left to rely on was her faith in God. She never quit believing in God's love and she never quit trusting him. She has adjusted as well as she can to her new circumstances and has done so without complaint. I had the privilege of meeting Elisabeth last spring, and I wonder now if that day I met one of this generation's heroes of the faith. Sometimes God takes away several legs of support from under us so that we will learn to lean on only him.

When tough times come we find out what we're made of. We have the choice of facing our problems, working through them and leaning on God, or running from all our responsibilities.

My grandparents have always been great gardeners. When I was younger and went to visit, the first thing I would do was run to the backyard and look at all the vegetables, fruits, and flowers that were growing there. My grandparents often had to scold me because I would try to eat the strawberries before they were ripe.

God can grow a beautiful garden of blessings from our seeds of disappointment. Flowers of trust, faith, patience, endurance, dependence on God, and dozens of other blessings can bloom from these trials. The more seeds or types of disappointments we are facing, the more flowers will grow in our garden.

When my classmate Anna began to sing that solo, I had the choice of how to respond. I could accept what had happened or become angry and bitter. I believe that because I chose to pray for the wisdom to make the best of it, the Lord granted me the opportunity of working at the TV station, where I learned much about my calling in life. The garden of blessings he had planned for me was beyond anything I could have imagined. You have a garden of blessings waiting to bloom for you, if you will endure the hard times. Your response when you are laid low will determine how high you can go.

Some of the Bible's most admired heroes went through times of utter despair. Job lost his family, his wealth, and his health. Even his friends turned on him, all at the same time. The Bible says that through all of his pain, "Job did not sin in what he said" (Jb 2:10). As a young teenager, Daniel was taken away from his family and became a prisoner of war in a foreign land that worshipped false gods. Even through all that suffering, he "purposed in his heart" that he would serve God (Dn 1:8, KJV). Both Job and Daniel responded by facing their problems, working through them, and leaning on God. Their responses determined their blessings.

One of my all-time favorite books is Corrie ten Boom's *The Hiding Place*. The book tells her story of hiding Jews in Holland during World War II. Eventually, the hiding place was suspected and Corrie and her family were arrested.

Corrie and her sister Betsie were sent to several prisons, including the infamous Ravensbruck concentration camp near Berlin. Corrie's father, a brother, another sister, and a nephew were sent to other prisons. In the camps, Corrie had a mighty ministry to the women who surrounded her. It would have been quite easy to become bitter, yet she chose to look at her disappointing circumstances and see the opportunity hidden within. I was especially impressed when Corrie said that she was thankful for the lice that infested their beds and clothing. Due to the infestation, the guards avoided their barracks, allowing Corrie and her sister to hold Bible studies. Corrie truly understood the blessings that come from disappointments.

God Bless the Smarte Cart

The Lord desires for each of his children to grow strong in the faith. The pathway to growth leads through many disappointments, trials, and despair. Kent Crockett, in *The 911 Handbook*, speaks about heavy burdens: "Jesus referred to this state of the soul as being 'weary and heavy-laden.' The accumulation of numerous burdens always brings heavy pressure on our souls. That's why Jesus said we could find rest for our souls if we would come to him."[1]

To produce patience, strength, and endurance in our lives, God often allows us to carry just enough heavy burdens to cause us to struggle. When I think about this, I picture myself lugging too many suitcases through an airport. I admit that when I travel I tend to overpack. (I think that perhaps it has to do with my shoe obsession.) I usually struggle to the counter with more bags than I can carry. My father can pack everything neatly into one bag and board the airplane with nothing but a magazine. I don't know how he does it! I usually struggle with two carry-ons and two or three huge suitcases.

My favorite item at the airport is the little Smarte Cart

dispenser. A Smarte Cart is a little metal cart with wheels that you can load your bags onto and push around the airport. Jesus is like that cart, and prayer is like the coins that we put into the machine to release the cart. Yes, he has given us many burdens to carry, but at any time in our struggle we can "cast our cares" on him and he will give us rest (1 Pt 5:7, KJV). Think of this analogy as you read what Jesus said: "Come to me, all who are weary and heavy-laden, and I will give you rest. Take my yoke upon you, and learn from me, for I am gentle and humble in heart; and you will find rest for your souls. For my yoke is easy and my burden is light" (Mt 11:28-30).

You may be carrying a lot of burdens right now, but God is there, waiting to give you rest if you'll only ask.

Prayer Starters

List any disappointments that have overwhelmed you lately.

_____

_____

What are some reasons why God may have allowed these things in your life?

_____

_____

What are some specific lessons you have learned through hard times?

_____

_____

What are some ways you can put your hope in God during times of despair?

_____

_____

Scripture Assignment
Psalm 42; Philippians 4:4; James 4:8

A Prayer for When Everything Goes Wrong

Dear sovereign Lord,

I feel like everything is crashing down around me and only you and I remain. It is so hard for me to accept all of these heartaches and learn from them. It is especially hard for me to pray when everything seems to be going wrong. Help me to stay close to you during rough times because you alone will never disappoint me. Show me the meaning of endurance and grow within me a garden of blessings from these seeds of disappointment.

In your Son's name,

Amen

FIVE

When You Feel Like a Failure

I've always loved artistic activities and all types of competition. That's why I was especially lucky that my Christian high school participated in a national fine arts competition each year. There were all sorts of exciting categories, like choir, art, creative writing, and drama. The first step of competition was to be chosen by your school to participate at a state level. If you placed first at the state level you then attended the nationals, which were usually held in Greenville, South Carolina.

I had been involved in choir and different drama presentations at my school, but one category in the competition that intrigued me more than the rest was Bible teaching. The rules were pretty simple: I had to present a Bible lesson to the judges as if they were children.

My sophomore year I won at the state level. I was thrilled. Next I competed at the national level, but lost there. Of course, I was just happy to have won state!

My junior year I tried again, hoping to go even further. Again I won for the state of North Carolina and competed in nationals, this time placing second. I was very excited, and determined then and there that my senior year would be my chance to take first place at the national level.

My senior year came, and everyone at my school—including me—was sure that I was going to go all the way. This was my year to take first at nationals and make my school proud!

When the time came for them to announce the winners at the state level I was poised to stand. It was a no-brainer; I'd already won two years in a row. They did indeed read my name, but it was for the alternate position. My senior year I didn't even win at the state level! I felt like a total failure. I had been to nationals twice, placing once, and now I had fallen on my face in a very public way.

Sometimes disappointments come despite doing our best, and sometimes in our failures we disappoint ourselves. Sometimes our "failures" aren't even failures at all. How do we deal with failure—and perceived failure? How do we keep it from consuming our present and controlling our future?

Look at Failure Differently

One of the greatest lessons my parents ever taught me was that at some point in my life, I would fail. No doubt, it would happen more than once. (Sometimes it feels like it happens all the time!) If you are human, you will fail, too. As children of God, we need not feel ashamed or isolated in our failure. The failures you and I experience can be anything: a flunked history test, a broken relationship, a hidden sin—even a lost competition. In any case, you and I are not alone.

When we fail, we often feel guilty, ashamed, angry with ourselves, and hurt that God could let us fail. Yet we have an opportunity to decide how to view our failure. We can say, "I tried and failed. I give up." Or we can say, "That hurt, but I'm going to try again." The specific response is up to us. We can choose to look at our failure as a stepping-stone to success and not as something that will hold us down indefinitely.

Have you ever looked through the wrong end of a pair of binoculars? When you look through the binoculars correctly, things that are far away appear much closer to you. However, if you look through the binoculars backward, your target object looks much smaller and you see more of its surroundings. Looking at it backward, you realize how your object compares in size to everything around it.

We can try to look at our failure in this way. We can view our failure against the background of eternity. My parents would often help me "flip the binoculars around" when I dealt with problems in high school. If I came home upset because of something that someone said, my parents would remind me that high school would last only four years, not the rest of my life. They would fill in the background for me and suddenly my problem wouldn't seem so overwhelming.

The writing world is filled with failure. Most authors can tell you how many rejections they received before finally getting a book contract. My mother has wanted to write for as long as I can remember. She worked for eleven years on various books, with little luck. After all of her hard work, and countless rejections, she finally received a contract to write Christian greeting cards for Lawson Falle, Ltd. She now finds that writing cards is more fulfilling to her than writing books. She has had the privilege of writing cards for Zig Ziglar, Dr. Mel Cheatham, and Franklin Graham. God knew what he was doing all the time. God said "No," because he had something better in mind.

Set Up Camp Somewhere Else

On one very normal day, I went to my mailbox and received an invitation to participate in a preliminary interview for a Miss Teen Raleigh pageant. I had never competed in a pageant in my life. Luckily, I'd had a few modeling classes that would help me appear as though I knew what I was doing even when I did not. I decided there was nothing to lose, so I went for the preliminary interview. I had a very relaxed and enjoyable interview and thought that as long as I was having fun, it was worthwhile. After the interview, I got my casual-wear outfit together and all the other things I needed. When the pageant night came, I won! I still have the pageant video, in which you can see my mouth drop open in surprise. Every other runner-up was quite poised and graceful; then there was me with my jaw on the floor, grinning like an idiot.

I went to the national pageant in Orlando that Christmas and competed against ninety-nine other girls. Miss America doesn't have to deal with those odds! All of us were standing on stage when they named the top ten. I was not one of them. The curtain closed behind the top ten and in front of all the rest. I remember disappointment washing over me, but I also remember thinking that I didn't deserve to be there in the first place. I was saddened, but deep inside I knew that I was lucky to be behind that curtain at all.

I turned around from my mark to see eighty-nine amazing young women crying. I don't remember seeing one without tears. It is intimidating to witness that many girls, all six feet tall, sobbing. After the announcement, I packed up my stuff and my family and I went to dinner. When the hostess asked how many were in my party, I felt like saying, "two adults and a loser for dinner." I felt defeated but I tried to focus on my family and the future.

The next day, as we walked out of the hotel lobby, I noticed two girls whose eyes were still swollen with tears. In that moment I realized that I could be crying, too, if I chose to dwell on the disappointment.

If you and I set up camp right in the middle of our failures, that is where we will stay. The best way to move on is to accept the failure, pull up our tent pegs, and move on. Replaying the failure repeatedly in our minds only prolongs the pain.

Watch Your Language

When we fail, we also can choose what type of language we will use as we respond to our setback. Will we use words like "quit" and "give up," or will we use words like "try again" and "persevere"?

In August 2001, the world was shocked to hear that a tragic plane crash had taken the life of singer and entertainer Aaliyah. In a television show about her life, I learned that she had been singing for much longer than I had realized. She sang a long time before she hit it big. Undoubtedly she had learned the lesson contained in one of her songs, "Try again." In this song, she encourages the listener not to give up on his or her dreams, but to "pick yourself up" and try again.

Dr. John C. Maxwell calls the process of using our failures to help us succeed "failing forward." In his book by the same name, he says, "Ninety percent of all those who fail are not actually defeated. They simply quit."[1] When I read that, I thought of the old saying, "Winners are just losers who got mad." Failure is such a crushing experience that we think that the answer has to be complex and difficult, but this is not the case. The way to overcome failure is simple: don't quit! "And let us not be weary in well doing: for in due season we shall reap, if we faint not" (Gal 6:9, KJV).

In *Tough Times Never Last, But Tough People Do*, Robert Schuller shares this story about quitting:

> A father once said to his boy, "Son you gotta set a goal and never quit. Remember George Washington?"
>
> The son said, "Yes."
>
> "Jefferson?"
>
> "Yes."
>
> "Abraham Lincoln?"
>
> "Yes."
>
> "You know what they all had in common?"
>
> "What?"
>
> The father said, "They didn't quit. Remember Ozador McIngle?"
>
> The kid said, "No. Who was he?"
>
> "See, you don't remember him. He quit!"[2]

Think About It

Strangely enough, we have a better chance of succeeding if we have failed at least once. When I was little, I used to ride my bicycle in our neighborhood. There are many bike crashes in my history. After a crash, I would sit up wherever I was—whether it was the sidewalk, the ditch, or someone's lawn—and just think. I would sit there and try to figure out what had gone wrong. Did I take the hill too fast? Did I turn the corner too sharply? Was there something wrong with my bike that caused the crash? I would also take a few minutes to look around and examine the damage that the crash had caused. I would not get back on the bike until I had analyzed the crash in its entirety.

When you fail, you can take some time to do the same. What went wrong? What measures can you take to prevent this in the future? What are the results of this failure? Ask God to help you learn from your failure. He has something to teach you. When you fail, it is important to get back up. Yet while you are down, take a few minutes to think.

Up and At 'Em

As the Lord was preparing me to write this book, I went through a number of disappointments. It has been amazing how God has allowed specific types of disappointment to come into my life at the very times that I was writing about them. During one particular week, I experienced three severe heartaches at college. My scholarship was not renewed, I was not rehired for a student government position, and I was not accepted into a new organization at school. Taken by themselves, these don't seem too overwhelming, but I was still dealing with the loss of my grandmother and the loss of some close friendships. As a group, these disappointments were crushing.

What could I do? There was only one thing to do. Hold fast to God and trust him for the next step. "My flesh and my heart may fail, but God is the strength of my heart and my portion forever" (Ps 73:26).

Prayer Starters

What has happened lately to make you feel like a failure?

_____

_____

_____

Describe to God how you feel about your "failure."

_____

_____

_____

What do you think God could help you learn through this experience?

_____

_____

_____

_____

Scripture Assignment
2 Corinthians 12:9

A Prayer for When You Feel Like a Failure

Dear almighty Father,

Even though I am your child, I feel like a loser right now. My hopes were so high and now they've come crashing down. I know I can't defeat my feelings without your help. I must remember that you can use my failures to help me in the future. Father, be with me right now. Only you can pick me up when I fall. Guide my actions and thoughts. Please use all the disappointments I go through for your glory.

In Jesus' name,

Amen

SIX

When Divorce Hits

I was exhausted. I had spent a long day at a writer's conference in Atlanta and my feet were aching. All I wanted to do was get into my swimsuit and jump into the hotel pool. No more people, no more walking—just refreshing water. Yet, as is often the case in my life, God had other plans.

I put my towel down on an empty chair and eased my way into the cool water.

SPLASH!

A young boy greeted me with a cannonball and quickly decided I was friend material.

"Hi, what's your name?" he said after he came up for air.

"Brittany. What's yours?" I looked around irritably. I was trying so hard to be polite, but this kid was standing in the way of my relaxing swim.

"Brandon. How old are you?" He started to put his over-sized snorkeling mask back on.

"I'm nineteen."

"Wow, you don't look nineteen. You look fifteen."

Just what every college girl wants to hear. His comment did not endear me to this kid. However, it was my turn to talk so I answered by smiling as politely as I could and asking how old he was.

"Oh, I just turned thirteen. I'm here with my mom. She works here at the conference. My dad used to work with us, too, but not anymore." His face dropped.

"Why doesn't your dad help anymore, Brandon?" Now I was honestly concerned.

"My mom and dad got a divorce six months ago. It has been really, really hard. I live in Texas, and when you are thirteen in Texas, you are considered legal by the state."

I was terribly ashamed at my earlier impatience with him.

"What are you legal for?"

"To decide. I have to choose which parent to live with." He took a deep breath and dived under the water, giving me a moment to ponder what he'd said.

How could this be? The poor kid was having a hard enough time with the divorce, but now he had to choose between his two parents. I could not possibly imagine something so painful, but he seemed to be dealing with it as well as could be expected.

Knowing I had to write this chapter, I asked Brandon what advice I should give to other teens who were dealing with divorce. Amazingly, his response was more positive than I ever would have imagined. He looked up at me with his warm brown eyes and said, "Tell them it will be OK. That their life is not over. It hurts, but it does get better." Wherever Brandon is right now, my prayers are with him and the difficult decision he had to make.

When Devastation Strikes

According to an article by Debbie Barr that appeared in *Discipleship Journal*, two out of every five American kids are children of divorce. In this article, entitled "Helping Children of

Divorce," the impact of divorce on a child is described.

"To a child, divorce is an emotional earthquake. It is a crisis so profound that only parental death ranks higher among childhood traumas. Actually, divorce is a 'death.' As such, it produces grief in the heart of every child it touches."[1]

Divorce is a devastating occurrence whose effects are felt long after the legal documentation is filed and signed. Emotions of all kinds swirl around inside its victims, leaving them dizzy and confused. In *How to Blend a Family*, Carolyn Johnson shares some of the emotions involved in divorce. "These emotional hurdles—grief, anger, fear, and loss of self-esteem—are not limited to the adult victims of divorce. Our children suffer the same emotions and follow a similar path in their transition from one family to another."[2]

A year or two ago, I was having one of those days in high school when everything goes wrong. I had gotten a bad grade on a test and I had forgotten my lunch. I was carpooling home with my good friend and her mother, who worked at the school. When we got out to the car my hands were full, so I put my brand-new Five Star First Gear notebook on the roof of the van for a moment. I got everything in the van and we took off for home.

As we pulled out onto a four-lane highway next to my school, I noticed my notebook was missing. I searched quickly for it, but couldn't find it anywhere. Just then, my friend, Kim, said, "I think I found it." She pointed out the back window and there was my notebook, lying flat on the highway. We watched it for a second before a semi-truck ran over it. We turned around to get it, but by the time we got there only shreds of my notebook remained. My homework, my graded papers, my permission slips, and all my class notes were swirling around the highway with each passing car. I could not believe it. I had gone from having everything organized and in my possession to losing it all in one moment.

Divorce hits lives like that semi-truck hit my notebook. All of a sudden, everything we thought was in order is in pieces. We are left looking at the devastated remains. This devastation can have lasting effects on our lives if we do not handle it properly.

Express Your Feelings

I love watching the old movie channels, like AMC (American Movie Classics) and TMC (The Movie Channel). I could sit all day on a couch with those on. My dad and I watch the old westerns whenever we get a chance. In every one, someone gets shot with an arrow or a bullet. The first thing the characters in the movie do is to call the town doctor to come remove the object. This is just gruesome! Using no anesthetic other than whiskey, doctors perform surgery wherever they happen to be. I can't stand to watch!

Sadly, the pain that is the result of divorce is like one of those deadly bullets. It must come out. The only way to get the pain out is to express our feelings. No matter how uncomfortable or painful, we must express the pain or it will continue to cause us harm. Just as an unattended bullet could end the life of one of those old-time cowboys, buried emotional pain can cause emotional and spiritual pain and death in our lives.

First of all, your parents need to know your feelings about their decision. Although it is tempting to yell out of anger or bitterness, you must fight the urge to blow up at them. Tell them calmly and rationally how you feel and how their decision will affect you. Do not expect them to change their decision based on what you tell them, but respectfully confront them with the result of that decision from your perspective.

Make sure that you are clear that these are your feelings, not a judgment. Some parents may see such communication as a challenge to their authority or an attempt to shame them. Make sure you don't push them too hard. They are probably feeling pretty terrible, too. Be honest, but be as gentle as you can be. You may want to say something like, "Mom (or Dad), I want us to have an open and healthy relationship, and I think that you do, too. I am telling you how I feel and how this affects me because I love you. You are one of the most important people in my life and I want us to keep the lines of communication open. I don't want this to come between us."

Our parents aren't the only ones to whom we need to talk. It is also incredibly important that we tell God how we are feeling through the whole process. It is easy to become angry with God as well, but communication keeps us close to the source of our only hope for peace. "The Lord is close to the broken-hearted and saves those who are crushed in spirit" (Ps 34:18). You probably know that God didn't cause this pain for you. If you do feel angry with him, though, tell him. Nothing can ever be kept secret from him, so you're not telling him anything that he doesn't already know! Often, telling God that we are angry with him is the first step in allowing ourselves to feel close to him again. Try to remember, he's not far away from you—even if it feels as though he is. He's right there with you, waiting for you to reach out to him.

Other ways of expressing pain could be to tell a close friend or relative, to write in a journal, or to express yourself artistically, perhaps painting or songwriting. There are many things you can do with the pain to prevent it from harming you further.

Avoiding the Parent Trap

I grew up watching the old Disney movies. *The Parent Trap* was one of my favorites. This movie was about twins who were separated at birth and each one given to a different parent, following a divorce. The twins eventually find each other at summer camp, then set in motion a plan to get their parents back together.

The movie is very funny and I even enjoyed the remake. Unfortunately, however, this is not real life. Children who suffer through a parent's divorce can spend years obsessing about getting their parents back together—to no avail. Although divorced people can be reconciled and remarried, it does not happen often. It is best if we just accept the change and, though it is hard, do the best we can to adapt to a new way of life.

A divorce is never a child's fault and it is not the child's responsibility to fix his or her parents' divorce. That is a matter between God and the couple. I know it is hurtful to think about your parents' separation, but only God can give you the strength to deal with such a heavy burden. As much as you want it to, taking matters into your own hands will not help.

My Friend Is Dealing With Divorce

In the past four years of our friendship, I had noticed that my friend Todd's parents did not interact well with one another but I did not know it would come down to this.

Todd and I grew up together in the youth group and Sunday school classes of my church. We talked almost every day for three years. In all that time, I noticed that Todd and his mom really were good friends.

Then Todd graduated and he learned that his parents were getting a divorce. His parents said they didn't love each other anymore. Todd had few people in his life with whom he could share this burden. He cried in my arms on more than one occasion. His whole life view changed. Every good family memory felt like a big joke. He was headed off to college, but what did he have to come home to? How could his parents just not love one another anymore? How could God let this happen?

The first thing we can do for a friend who is dealing with his or her parents' divorce is to show support. If one of your friend's parents died, you would most likely send flowers and cards, call your friend, or even go by and visit. When a loved one dies, there is a flood of sympathy and support. Yet when someone's parents get divorced we usually don't do anything. We have already seen that a child deals with the same feelings in divorce that they would in death; therefore, it is equally important to show our love and support during this time. I know that it can be intimidating to talk to your friend about an issue such as this, but believe me, your friend will appreciate and remember how much you cared.

Next, you should make yourself available to listen. Sometimes your friend will feel like talking about the situation and at other times he or she will look to his or her friends as an escape from the pain. You must be sensitive to what your friend needs. Let your friend know that you are there to listen if he or she needs to talk. Your friend may talk about the situation for hours, or he or she may never bring it up. In either case, you have made yourself available to listen.

Finally, you should keep your friend and his or her family in your prayers. Oftentimes we remember our friends' pain in our prayers when these situations first hit, but forget to give them prayer support a couple of weeks or months later. Divorce is an ongoing process. The healing does not come quickly or easily. Keep up that intercession for your friend.

How can we even describe in words the pain of a broken family? How can we deal with a life that is completely opposite to the one we knew and loved? Only through God can we do the impossible. His love is bigger even than the pain of divorce. People disappoint us, but God never will. "Though my father and mother forsake me, the Lord will receive me" (Ps 27:10).

Prayer Starters

How do you feel when you hear the word "divorce"?

_____

_____

_____

_____

_____

How has your relationship with God changed as a result of this divorce?

_____

_____

_____

_____

_____

How can you show your love and support to a friend who is dealing with divorce?

_____

_____

_____

_____

_____

Scripture Assignment
1 John 2:7-9; Psalm 10:14

A Prayer for When Divorce Hits

Gracious Savior,

My whole world is splitting apart. My parents have gotten a divorce. I am totally helpless as I watch everything change. I don't understand why or how this happened. I cling to you, Father, as I cry these tears. Only you know how painful this is for me.

Help me treat each parent in a loving and respectful way, even if I don't agree with what has happened. I believe that you can bring good from painful experiences and I ask you to do that for me. I need your Spirit here with me as I deal with the changes in my life.

In your loving arms,

Amen

SEVEN

When You Lose a Loved One

For spring break of my sophomore year at college, I spent a whole week with ten friends in San Diego. We had an amazing time! We played on the beaches, shopped at the malls, ate at great restaurants, and even took a trip to Mexico. What great memories!

When I stepped off the plane back in Ohio, where I go to school, my parents were waiting for me. Though this was completely unexpected, I did not assume that there was anything wrong. I thought they had traveled up from North Carolina to see me for my birthday, which was in early April. As they approached, I could see that my mother had been crying. Something was very wrong. My mother put her arm around me and softly said, "Your grandma has passed away."

I was stiff with shock and grief. My grandma was one of my best friends. She was more than a grandmother; she was and will always be my biggest cheerleader. We had talked twice on the phone during my trip to San Diego. I had a postcard in my purse I had written to her that day. It was Sunday night. Grandma had passed away on Friday due to a heart attack. My parents didn't tell me right away because I would have come back from my trip early; I would have been alone on my flight, crying the whole way.

Within twenty-four hours I was at the funeral home, looking at my beautiful grandmother, dressed in an outfit that my mother and I had picked out for her. I could not stop crying.

The rest of the family cried intermittently, because they'd already had a few days to grieve, but my tears were constant. My reaction to the pain was utterly uncontrollable. I could see that she had just painted her fingernails. She always painted them before trips.

It has been four months since that day, but my pain is still fresh. At the same time, I am able to cope with life and to enjoy happy memories of the times I shared with my grandmother and friend.

A lot of us are raised to believe that strong people don't cry or that we are supposed to "get over" painful experiences quickly. Nothing could be further from the truth! When you lose someone you love, let yourself grieve. Don't bottle it up. Don't try to be strong. Don't pretend it isn't happening. Had I not wept on and off for months, sometimes even lying on the floor of my dorm room, I would not be healthy right now.

How Do You Let Yourself Grieve?

When I think of grief, I think of it as communicating the loss I feel. By communicating, I mean praying, journaling, or crying on the shoulder of a friend. It is important to get grief out. If we keep it inside, our health will suffer and we will face the battle of bitterness.

In the midst of my grieving over my grandmother's death, my good friend Matt called. I thought at first that it would be the typical, "I am sorry for your loss" kind of call, but I was surprised. He told me one of the most valuable things anyone could have said. He said, "Britt, write it down." I am a constant journaler, but Matt knew that when overwhelming situations hit me I stop writing. I started journaling again right after that call, and I cannot describe how much it helped.

Friends and loved ones are essential to helping you communicate your grief. I had amazing friends at school that wrote me letters, called to check on me, and even offered to take me off campus to get my mind off things. It's tempting to withdraw when you are in a lot of pain, but do not forsake your friends during this time; embrace them. Jesus himself asked three friends to help him deal with his sorrow in the Garden of Gethsemane. "He took Peter, James, and John along with him and he began to be deeply distressed and troubled. 'My soul is overwhelmed with sorrow to the point of death,' he said to them. 'Stay here and keep watch'"(Mk 14:33-34). He didn't ask his friends to explain God's will or give him all the answers. He simply asked them to "stay." Being with your friends is a great comfort in itself.

Listen to God

In times of loss, it is easy to look toward heaven, not with tears in our eyes, but with anger in our hearts. How could God let this happen? Why didn't he let this person live long enough for me to have one more conversation with her, or one more hug? Why didn't I have a chance to say goodbye? Why didn't I ever stop to tell him how much I loved him?

In reality, no matter how long this person might have lived, we would always want more. We may never know exactly why God took our loved one when he did. Yet we can be sure that he had a reason and a purpose. Zig Ziglar, in his book *Confessions of a Grieving Christian,* shares the words of Reverend Jim Lewis, who spoke at the funeral of Zig Ziglar's daughter, Susan Ziglar Witmeyer.

In the mysteries of life there is going to be a day when the end of God's glorious plan will justify all the mysterious means that He has used in accomplishing His plan and purpose on this earth.

Why? Have you ever said, "You know, I'm going to ask God about that one when I get to heaven. I need to find out what was behind all of that?" You know what I suspect? When we get to heaven and we see Jesus in all of His glory, in all of His majesty, in all of His splendor, there will be but two words that we will say concerning the questions of life: "Of course." One glimpse of Him will be all that we shall need for the rest of eternity concerning the mysteries of life.[1]

On that day we will understand fully, but not until then will we know.

Despite the pain it causes, death also has much to give. This is because death is a teacher like no other. After someone you love dies, suddenly you see time, people, and your own life differently. Hidden in this black, choking cloud of loss are glistening drops of wisdom that God wants us to glean. If we turn ourselves away from God we will miss the gifts he wants to give us through our experience, and the loss will be for no purpose. Through every step of this excruciating process it is important for us to listen to God.

Let Go of Guilt

I should have called one more time. I should have mailed that postcard at the beginning of the week. I should have gone to Florida to be with her instead of to San Diego. I should have told her so many things that I'll never have the chance to tell her. I should have ... I should have ... I feel so guilty.

If you let yourself run with the "I should have's," they will never stop.

One day while I was on vacation with my family in Gatlinburg, Tennessee, I was taking a walk around our hotel when I looked down through a metal grate toward the parking lot below. One of the most beautiful butterflies I have ever seen was just below the grate. It was bright yellow and black and full of life. I watched it flutter for a few minutes but soon it ran into the grate, trying to get out of the garage. I knew that only a few feet from the butterfly was a large opening through which it could easily escape. I continued watching the butterfly, growing more and more frustrated that I could not help it. The butterfly struggled as if caged when it was actually free. Guilt is like that. It is a cage into which we put ourselves, when we actually have already been released. We are free because God is in control of our lives. He knew exactly how many times I should have talked to my Grandma before she died. He knew when the best time was for her to go.

Ephesians 1:11b says that God "worketh all things after the counsel of his own will" (KJV). God not only makes a plan for our lives and the lives of others, he consistently works out that plan. We can be free from "should have's" because God is our Father, and he knows what is best for us all along the way.

Live Life

At first it may be very beneficial to stop your daily activities and do nothing but grieve, but such times should not be prolonged. Erwin Lutzer describes this in *Managing Your Emotions.*

> One of the most important things you can do in a time of sorrow is to continue, as much as possible, the normal activities that force you to make decisions. This will help you orient yourself to your new life without the loved one. Even if you do not have to go to work on a job, it is important to keep up activities at home that will move you forward. Inactivity lets you dwell too much on the tragedy.[2]

While I was in Gatlinburg recently, I visited Ripley's Aquarium. One of their most fascinating sites is a long, glass, underwater tunnel through which people can walk as sharks swim right over their heads. It was surreal. One of the things I noticed was that the sharks never quit swimming. One of the guides there told us that some types of shark have to keep moving to breathe. If they quit swimming, they will sink to the bottom of the tank and suffocate. Living through grief is like that. If we put everything on hold, we could sink. We must keep swimming.

After Grandma passed away, I did not want to return to college for the last quarter of the school year. I didn't want to go to class, hang out with friends, or do anything. Those are things you do when life is OK, and my life was *not* OK. I wanted to go home, but that was not an option. I knew that would put me behind academically, and my parents would not have encouraged it. I had to fight those feelings of wanting to give up on everything. I had to *work* at doing normal activities. It has taken many months, but now I don't have to work as hard. I am so glad now that I did not leave school. I needed to get back to life. I had to keep moving or I would have become frozen in my grief. I had to swim.

Learn From Your Loved One

The Bible says, "Honor all men" (1 Pt 2:17, KJV). One of the best ways to honor those who have gone to heaven before us is to learn from them. I observed godly principles in my grandfather and grandmother and have tried to walk in those spiritual footsteps ever since. I journaled these lessons that I observed in them both and continually challenge myself with them. Here are a few from my list:

I never heard my grandfather speak badly of anyone— "Speak evil of no man"(Ti 3:2, KJV).

He always believed the best of people—"Love ... believeth all things" (1 Cor 13:7, KJV).

My grandma gave without measure and always supported my ministry—"God loveth a cheerful giver" (2 Cor 9:7, KJV).

I hope to leave this same legacy to my children one day. What are the spiritual lessons you have learned from your loved ones? Can you find Scripture passages that parallel what they have taught you?

Another way we can learn from the loss of our loved ones is to cherish the time we have left with others who are still with us. When my grandfather died, right before my senior year of high school, I truly began to appreciate my grandmother. I spent a lot of time with her during grandpa's sickness, and I was even there to weep with her when she received the phone call that he had died. When she left to go home after weeks of being with me, I missed her. Not like missing a distant grandparent, it was like missing a true friend. From that point on, I called, wrote, and visited her more frequently. I had realized what James meant when he wrote, "What is your life? It is even a vapor, that appeareth for a little time, and then vanisheth away" (Jas 4:14b, KJV).

Time is precious. Make it count with those you love.

Prayer Starters

How did you feel when you first heard that your loved one had passed away?

_____

_____

_____

Do you ever feel guilty about "should have's"?

_____

_____

What spiritual lessons has God taught you through the life of your loved one?

_____

_____

_____

_____

Scripture Assignment
Psalm 23; Job 42

A Prayer for When You Lose a Loved One

Lord of heaven and earth,

Words cannot express the feelings and emotions that I am experiencing right now. My life has been forever altered by the loss of _____. I don't understand many things, including why you have decided to take my loved one's life now, but I do know that one day I will understand completely. Until then, give me the grace to continue living every day for your glory. Give me peace as I wrestle with this gripping grief. May I learn from my loved one's life and may I make my loved one proud. Thank you for being a constant source of comfort.

In your hands,

Amen

EIGHT

When You Have Unsaved Loved Ones

I first met Claire during my freshman year of college, and I have become very close to her. She is quite a remarkable Christian. She accepted the Lord into her life at a young age and grew up in a church where she learned about the Bible.

After her first year of college, Claire started working at a coffee shop near another large university. One day a homeless man came into the shop and randomly asked Claire if she could read the Bible to him. He could not read, nor did he have a Bible of his own. He did not know Claire or know that she was a Christian. Claire gladly read to the man from her Bible and was able to share her faith with him.

Though Claire easily shares God's light with strangers, her greatest struggle is sharing God with a loved one. Her Aunt Lisa owns the coffee shop in which she works. Claire is so close to Lisa that they consider each other sisters. Lisa grew up in a church that taught that one simply had to be a good person to go to heaven. She does not understand that because God is holy and cannot embrace sin, none who have sinned can ever be good enough to reach him on our own. She doesn't grasp the importance of the miracle that took place when God's Son, Jesus, came to earth, died for our sins, and was resurrected, all so that we can be forgiven of sin and promised a spot in heaven. Lisa does not listen when Claire speaks of Jesus and salvation because she thinks that she is already good enough. Claire knows that none of us can be that good. Claire loves Lisa so much that the thought of not being with her one day in heaven is almost crippling. She and her family continue to pray that one day Lisa will understand the truth and enter into a saving relationship with Jesus Christ.

Having an unsaved loved one in your life is a heavy burden to carry. Many Christians find themselves in this place. Maybe you do. I do, too. If we let ourselves, we could do nothing but worry all day long. It is very frustrating to know the truth but not be able to convince others of it. It is also frustrating to not understand what the other person believes.

Most likely there are people in your life who look saved but are not, and some who look unsaved but are. It isn't our place to judge a person's relationship with God. Only God can know the inner workings of a person's soul.

It's important for us to talk with our loved ones about God, because he is the most important thing in our lives, and we want to share what—or rather who—is in our hearts. We may also hope to open our family members or friends up to the Lord by sharing about him. No matter how much we would like to force God on our loved ones, however, we cannot. Yet there are some principles and tips that can help us when we do speak with our loved ones about God.

A Lesson From Jesus

John 4:1-38 records the story of Jesus and the woman at the well. Jesus came upon the woman and asked her for a drink of water. Jesus had no problem speaking with this woman, despite the fact that she was living in sin and was a Samaritan—

a group of people with whom Jews, like Jesus, were not supposed to associate. Using the well as a starting point for conversation, Jesus shared with the woman that he, being the Messiah, could give her *living* water that would forever satisfy her thirst—moving from her physical need for water to her spiritual need. Notice that Jesus was not judgmental or condemning of the woman. He could have shunned her for being immoral but he did not see only her sin. Jesus saw a child he loved. He cared for this woman and her soul.

Jesus teaches us an important lesson here: Love is our greatest magnet to draw others to God.

The first and most important thing we can do to draw our loved ones to Christ is to continue to love them unconditionally. I think that many Christians miss opportunities to draw others to Christ because they are too worried about the sin in the other person's life. Sometimes we are so concerned with telling another person that his or her lifestyle is wrong that we miss a chance to share God and his love. It is God's responsibility to change people; our responsibility is simply to love them.

Understand What You Can and Cannot Do

Do you remember the old saying, "You can lead a horse to water, but you can't make him drink"? That saying illustrates what we can and cannot do for our unsaved loved ones. We can share the gospel with our loved ones. We can lead them to the water of God's love. We can tell them how God has changed us. Yet we cannot force God into their lives.

In the book *People Sharing Jesus*, Darrell W. Robinson shares five principles for witnessing to a close friend or family member.

1. Be genuine in your communication.
2. Pray for the guidance of the Holy Spirit.
3. Convey a spirit of love, humility, and courtesy.
4. Avoid an attitude of condescension, judgment, and condemnation.
5. Ask for the person's permission.[1]

My friend Shari remembers that when she was in high school, she used to argue with a friend about which religion was right: Christianity or Mormonism. Finally, after years of arguing, Shari's Mormon friend said resolutely, "You've just convinced me more than ever that I'm right." Shari's motives were good: she wanted to see her friend learn to love Jesus. Yet debating didn't provide any evidence of Jesus' love. In fact, it only drove her friend in the opposite direction. Shari learned a painful but important lesson that day: God doesn't want us to attack our friends; he wants us to love them. He doesn't want us to change their minds; he wants us to touch their hearts.

God wants us to share his love with everyone we meet, but whether a person accepts God or not is up to him or her. "For it is by grace you have been saved, through faith—and this not from yourselves, it is the gift of God—not by works, so that no one can boast" (Eph 2:8-9).

It is heartbreaking to love someone who has not come to the Lord, but our greatest desire cannot make him or her accept Jesus. It is important to realize that God loves your loved ones as well and is working in their lives to draw them to him. "For God so loved the world that he gave his one and only Son, that whoever believes in him shall not perish but have eternal life" (Jn 3:16). God is working on your loved ones and he wants to use you to make the difference. Yet the weight of it doesn't rest entirely on your shoulders. You are simply a key part of what God is doing. Ultimately, he is the one who changes hearts.

Pray, Pray, Pray

Have you ever been put in a headlock by someone? I absolutely hate it. I hate the feeling that I have no control, that I am stuck.

I sometimes feel that way when I have shared the gospel with someone I care about and they have rejected it. I can't make anything happen. None of us can force someone into accepting the Lord. However, there is one thing we can do. We can pray.

It is easy to feel that our prayers are insignificant and useless. Because prayer is so simple, we imagine that it cannot be that powerful. Yet it most definitely is. Let's think about what prayer is. Prayer is going before the Creator and God of the universe and requesting something in the name of his Son. When we look at it from that perspective, it sounds a lot more important.

Don't be afraid to ask others to pray for your loved one as well. Can you imagine a baseball team with only one hitter? I would rather have a whole team batting than just one person. The same principle applies to prayer. Ask godly Christians around you to pray specifically and often for your loved one. Pray that the Holy Spirit will begin to work on that person's heart. Pray also that God will bring other Christians into that person's life so that he or she will become surrounded by the truth.

We must be consistent in our prayers. Praying for an unsaved loved one may take a week, ten years, or a lifetime. In any case, our responsibility is to pray. Never underestimate the power of prayer. "The prayer of a righteous man is powerful and effective" (Jas 5:16b).

Shine Out Your Light

Have you noticed that today's sitcom families are rather dysfunctional? Usually, one or both of the parents take on the attitude that the children should "do as I say, not as I do." What happened to the Cosby days, when the parents set a good example and the children followed?

Oftentimes we act like these TV families when it comes to our Christian testimony. We want to live our lives any way we please and still claim to be very close with God in front of our unsaved loved ones. Two and two must equal four to your friends and family. If they hear you speak of God and then see you living the way you did before you were saved, things will not add up. You and I need to be transformed before our loved ones in every area of life.

You are the light of the world. A city on a hill cannot be hidden. Neither do people light a lamp and put it under a bowl. Instead they put it on its stand, and it gives light to everyone in the house. In the same way, let your light shine before men, that they may see your good deeds and praise your Father in heaven.

MATTHEW 5:14-16

We must be consistent in our words, our actions, our dress, and the way we treat each other. The best witnessing tool any Christian possesses is the way he or she lives.

Make It Available

I use ketchup on just about everything I eat. When I was living at home, whenever I ran out of ketchup I would look around for a new bottle. If I didn't see another bottle in the cabinet I would use those little packets you get at fast food restaurants, which rarely open without a stuggle. Inevitably, I would be sitting at the table with a huge stack of empty ketchup packets when my mom would walk in, go to the cabinet, get out a fresh bottle, and set it right in front of me. It aggravated me every time. Because the new bottle wasn't easily available, I frustrated myself with the little packets.

When your loved one seeks the truth, it needs to be readily available to him or her. We all are drawn to the path of least resistance. If the gospel is not easily accessible, your loved one most likely will not embark on what feels like a wild goose chase to find it. It is your job as a Christian to make the gospel available. I don't mean that you should leave a Bible on every chair in the house. There are lots of natural ways to share the gospel. There are Christian books, CDs, and even movies that make great gifts to an unsaved person. In this way, you aren't shoving the gospel down his or her throat, but you are slipping it in. Your local Christian bookstore can be a great resource for you in this way.

Much more important, however, is the sharing of your life. Whenever you do something kind for someone, you are sharing the gospel. Whenever you open your heart, which is filled with God's love, you are sharing the gospel. Whenever you pass on a kind word, you are sharing the gospel. Whenever you are there for a friend in his or her pain or joy, you are sharing the gospel.

Another key way you can make the gospel available is to tell your unsaved loved one that you understand that he or she does not want to talk about it now, but that if he or she ever has any questions, to call you. In this way you are making yourself available without making yourself a nuisance.

You don't always have to get your loved ones to worship service on Sunday morning to expose them to the light of God's Word. Someone who would normally not attend church services may have no problem going with you to a Christian play or concert or a church picnic. Perhaps on some of these outings the gospel will be presented. Even if it is not, this gives your unsaved loved one a chance to interact with you and other Christians and observe your lives.

You might also consider inviting him or her to your home for dinner with you and a couple of your Christian friends— or just to hang out with you when you go to the movies or the mall. You will have to be careful about this approach, because you don't want the person to feel outnumbered or trapped, but you do want to expose him or her to God's love. Make sure you focus on loving the person, not on preaching at him or her. You will do more good with your love and acceptance than with anything that can come out of your mouth. Hospitality is something that most of us take for granted in today's world, but it is still a powerful tool in God's toolbox.

You Can Make a Difference

In the movie *Pay It Forward* a boy named Trevor is given an assignment by his social science teacher. In order to get credit for the assignment, he must find a way to change the world and put that plan into action. Trevor decides that his way of changing the world will be to do a favor for someone else and ask him or her not to pay it back but to pay it forward to three other people. The movie clearly teaches that each of us can make a tremendous difference in the world by helping just one other person.

You may not be able to witness to a whole country of people, or even convert an entire neighborhood, but you can change the world through one person. "But you will receive power when the Holy Spirit comes on you; and you will be my witnesses in Jerusalem, and in all Judea and Samaria, and to the ends of the earth." (Acts 1:8).

Prayer Starters

What is the hardest part about witnessing to a loved one?

_____

_____

_____

_____

_____

How has God challenged us by asking us to tell others about him?

_____

_____

_____

_____

_____

_____

What can you do to set a good example?

_____

_____

_____

_____

_____

_____

Scripture Assignment
2 Corinthians 2:14-17

A Prayer for When You Have Unsaved Loved Ones

Dear heavenly Father,

Thank you for your gift of salvation to all who would ask. We don't deserve any of your mercy. Father, it breaks my heart to think that _____ may not be with us one day in heaven. I know how gracious it was of you to save me, and I want to share that gift with so many. Please give me the wisdom and discernment I need in order to witness. Give me boldness and the right words to say. Help me to remember that it is my responsibility to love others, not to push them. Give me strength.

In your light,

Amen

NINE

When You Are Sick of Being Single

I love the show "MTV Cribs." In this show, the audience gets a personal tour of the homes of famous artists, actors, and performers. "Lifestyles of the Rich and Famous," which many of our parents watched, was the old school version of this show. The most interesting thing about "MTV Cribs" is hearing the homeowners talk about how they hired interior decorators to design their houses to meet their individual needs.

People need to be remodeled and updated, too. Every time we learn something, remodeling takes place within us. If I learn how to play chess for the first time, a new window of ability swings open inside me. If I learn to listen better, I learn to be a better friend. The remodeling takes place no matter what lesson is learned. It could be something as simple as playing tennis or as complex as true forgiveness.

Imagine that your room is going to be completely remodeled. We are talking new carpet, new paint, and the walk-in closet of your dreams. Your bags are packed and ready for your hotel stay, which will be necessary until these renovations are complete. The big day arrives and you call the hotel to check on your reservation. Disaster! Your reservation is nowhere to be found and you have to live at home during the whole renovation process. The workers can work on your room only during the day when you are at school because they need room to maneuver. They have to quit promptly when you return. You think to yourself, *This will take forever!*

When the room of your heart is occupied with a boyfriend or girlfriend, changes and modifications to your life also can be frustratingly slow. Think of how much quicker and easier they can be completed when God, the master interior decorator, has room to work. Although it is disappointing not to have a significant other in our lives, when we are single God can more easily come in and give our hearts a fresh start and a new look.

Webster's Dictionary for Everyday Use uses the term "single" to mean unmarried, among other definitions.[1] We are using "single" in this chapter in a broader sense. This chapter is for the unmarried young person, the teen without a boyfriend or girlfriend, or the teen that does not have permission to date at all. In every circumstance, loneliness can be a common thread.

Although loneliness is very painful, there are certain lessons we cannot learn unless we go through a time of singleness. How will we ever learn who we truly are if we do not first have time alone in which to find out? How can we learn that God alone is enough without having no one *but* God? How can we be reminded of the value of lasting friendships without needing to rely on our friends for companionship? We cannot comprehend certain experiences without living through singleness. Most importantly, there is a level of intimacy between God and his children that cannot be reached without this time. If you are single right now, you have been chosen by God to receive a free remodeling of your heart.

Many areas of our lives can be remodeled during this season of singleness, but we are going to review four major areas: spiritual, physical, intellectual, and emotional.

Spiritual Remodeling

Spiritual remodeling must always begin with God; he is the source of our spirituality and the reason we should want to grow.

Time Out With God

There is no bigger threat than dating to our devotional time with the Lord. Rebecca found this to be true when she began a relationship with Tony. She shares her struggle in one of her journal entries:

Dear God,

I am sorry that we haven't talked that much lately. I usually go out with Tony on the weekends and get back around midnight. By that time, I am so tired all I can do is fall asleep. On the weekdays, I do my homework until eight, and then I talk with Tony until eleven or so, when Mom makes me get off the phone. I do try after that to do my devotions, but I usually fall asleep during my prayers. Some lady at church suggested that I spend time with you in the morning, so I tried that. But you know, God, I have to get up so early to get ready for school. I have to pick out my clothes, take my shower, and do my hair and makeup. Tony likes it when I take extra time to look nice. I don't even get breakfast most days. Mornings are crazy around my house. I am sorry God. I will try to do better.

Rebecca

I know that it is painful to be lonely, but one good thing about singleness is that you will not be as tempted to skip out on your time with God. The truth is that practicing devotions regularly is difficult, whether you are single or not. It will probably always require discipline. If you are single you will have one less thing competing for your time with God. Take this opportunity to see how you can renew, regulate, and rediscover your communication times with the Lord.

Practicing Your Serve

It is important to serve God through your times of heartaches and trials. Singleness creates a great opportunity to do this. Being alone provides unique opportunities to serve God in the way he leads you. In the midst of that discipleship group, choir, soup kitchen, or Sunday school class, you will not feel so alone. The good news is that serving God will not only encourage you and help take your mind off of your singleness, it will also benefit many other people. Serving is doing something for God and for yourself, but also for the world.

I was fifteen the first time I experienced heartbreak and the loneliness of being single. Craig wanted to break up so that he could regain his singleness. I understood, but that didn't make it hurt less. That summer I started a church and community organization that worked with the Meals on Wheels program, visited rest homes, and ministered to the elderly of our church. During the very first week of working with this ministry, I felt better. I was not cured of my pain. Deep inside, I still wanted to curl up in my bed with a fuzzy blanket and listen to sad country music, but that desire lessened each time I made an older person smile. I felt better because I had a focus and a purpose.

Some of the greatest servants in the history of the church

were single. Joan of Arc and the well-known missionary Amy Carmichael were single; the famous author C.S. Lewis was a bachelor until age fifty-seven; Mother Teresa spent seven decades serving in India as a single woman. I am sure they were all very lonely at times, but they clearly found fulfillment in knowing and serving God. They certainly never let their singleness stand in their way of living a rich life. In fact, it was their singleness that allowed them to accomplish many of the deeds for which they are now known.

Remember our earlier definitions of singleness? Another definition of singleness found in *Webster's Dictionary for Everyday Use* is "honesty of purpose,"[2] which means to have a sincere purpose for your actions. What a perfect way to express what our hearts should be doing while we are single. Our "honesty of purpose" should be serving God.

Physical Remodeling

Spiritual remodeling should always come before our physical priorities, but it is also important to take care of our bodies. During the disappointing times of our lives, we are more susceptible to feeling down about ourselves or even becoming depressed. One way to guard against this is to take good care of our bodies. Exercise, rest, and good nutrition are the key players in this ballgame.

Of course, our outward appearance does not compare with our inward appearance, but we do represent the Lord with our image. I am not suggesting that we must look perfect, but I am saying that getting in shape and looking nice can go a long way in how we feel about ourselves. We all know vengeance is the Lord's, but looking great in front of an ex is a fun little feeling! Just keep in mind, this is not about getting her or him back, making your ex feel guilty, or getting another date on the rebound. This is about taking care of yourself and remembering how much you are worth.

Intellectual Remodeling

The more we grow intellectually, the more we realize that the world is so much bigger than ourselves. Expanding our intellect when we are single allows us to keep the right perspective on the world and grow as a person. It has been noted that very few of us in the Internet generation take time to read. Often we don't feel as though we need to take the time because of all the information that is easily available at our fingertips.

Whether or not someone reads also depends on whether he or she has time to do it. Maintaining a relationship with a dating partner takes up a lot of your free time. When you are single, you have that free time back. Why not read those books you have been meaning to read all along? Why not actually read that book from school, rather than doing the Cliffs Notes thing? You will never have a better opportunity to learn than when you are self-motivated and have the time. Richard Carlson, in his book *Don't Sweat the Small Stuff for Teens*, suggests reading a minimum of eight pages every day. Within a year, this will add up to three thousand pages! Think of the wisdom that can be gained from three thousand pages.[3] Expand your reading preferences. If you enjoy fiction, try a nonfiction book, the newspaper, or a magazine. There is a short reading list included at the back of this book, if you are stuck for ideas.

Expanding your horizons means more than just reading. You can join a sports team, check out a community service organization, or work as an intern at a nearby business. Remember, these are not means of escape. You need to face your loneliness head-on before any real healing can occur. However, keeping yourself occupied with healthy activities can be an important part of the healing process.

Emotional Remodeling

Healthy emotions are a prerequisite for starting a good relationship and for living a happy single life. When my friends come over, I have one condition for their visit: They must let me make them smoothies. My recipe is a simple one but it has become my specialty. I like making the smoothies; however, our blender is a bit temperamental. If you put a couple of large pieces of ice inside, they can sometimes get stuck.

Dealing with the aftermath of a breakup or learning complete trust in God is a little like dealing with those hard pieces of ice. The hard pieces of our lives must be broken down, dealt with, and blended before we can become the people God wants us to be. The best way I have learned to deal with those broken pieces is journaling.

Writing about the hard things in our lives and looking at them on paper helps us deal with our realities. When we learn to deal with our realities in light of God's work in our lives, we become emotionally healthy. Evaluating our emotions helps us to deal with them in the future. Hiding from our pain and distracting ourselves from it will not help. It will only hurt. Work through the how's and why's of your disappointment on paper, in conversations with friends, and in prayer. Looking at these shattered pieces will help you see the big picture of God's grace.

Only, But Not Lonely

I am an only child—not by my parents' choice but by God's. My mother had a miscarriage when I was two years old. As an only child I received certain advantages, just as children in large families receive other advantages. I benefited from my parents' undivided attention, I didn't get dragged into my siblings' problems, I wasn't distracted in any way from my own life lessons, and I was the only one for my parents to teach. If I had been one of ten siblings, I would have enjoyed different advantages.

When we are living life without a mate, fiancé, boy- or girlfriend, or even a romantic interest, God is the Father of an only child. How much more can he teach and mold us in his loving ways when we are his only children.

Earlier in this chapter, I mentioned Joan of Arc as one of God's famous single servants. In a George Bernard Shaw play entitled *Saint Joan,* Joan states, "Do not think you can frighten me by telling me that I am alone. France is alone; and God is alone; and what is my loneliness before the loneliness of my country and my God? ... Well, my loneliness shall be my strength too: It is better to be alone with God: His friendship will not fail me, nor His counsel, nor His love. In His strength I will dare, and dare, and dare, until I die."[4]

The first time I read that, I was single, without a boyfriend. (I am single right now, for that matter.) When I read Joan's statement, I wanted to run into the street, put my arms up like Rocky, and shout for joy. You are not the only single person, and how you view and deal with your singleness is your choice.

Go into your world and "dare, and dare, and dare until you die."

Prayer Starters

How do you feel about being single?

_____

_____

_____

What are some areas in your life that you want God to remodel?

_____

_____

_____

How has your relationship with God changed in your singleness?

_____

_____

_____

Scripture Assignment
1 Corinthians 7:32-35

A Prayer for When You Are Sick of Being Single

Dear Father,

I know that you have allowed me to be single right now for a reason, but it is getting harder and harder to be content. I know in my singleness I need to focus on serving you and growing as a person. Please use me for your glory in whatever way you see fit. Show me the areas in my life that need to be remodeled. Be with me right now as I feel so alone, Father. Comfort me and guide me in my singleness.

In your name,

Amen

TEN

When You Are Crushed by a Crush

My friend Rob had just decided to date a girl named Katie. It had occurred to me that they were going to end up together. I had known it for some time and I never thought twice about it. I thought Rob deserved a nice girl and I hoped Katie would be that for him.

Then one day I walked into class and saw Rob's arm around Katie. Yet it looked different than did most guys with their arm around a girl. Rob had a protective and appreciative gleam in his eye. I thought of how secure Katie must have felt.

After Rob and Katie got together, he and I continued our friendship as we always had. We even worked together on a few projects for school. Sometimes he would tell me about how badly Katie treated him. All the time Rob and I were working together I noticed the way he spoke of his family, the way he handled himself when a problem arose, and, most of all, how he earned respect from everyone around him. Over the months of his relationship with Katie, I began to admire and respect Rob even more than before.

One autimn day, I was chatting with him when out of the blue he told me that he and Katie had broken up. I truly was saddened that both Rob's and Katie's expectations had not been met. Yet, deep down, I was also glad that Rob was single again. I knew that the bond between Rob and Katie ran deep and that there was a good chance they would get back together.

I considered telling Rob how I felt about him but I worried that he would not have the same feelings toward me. I considered not saying anything, but I felt that if they got back together I would always regret not saying something. So I wrote him a letter. (I know, I know. I'm a coward!)

In the letter I said as delicately and gracefully as I could that I was interested in him. To my surprise, he wrote me back right away, explaining that he had wondered about me in the past but he knew that if God wanted us together he would put us together. He reminded me that we are ultimately not in control of our lives anyway.

In the end Rob and Katie did not get back together. Yet he did not pursue me, either. Sometimes crushes are crushing because the person does not want you. Sometimes crushes are crushing because you are left waiting without an answer. I am not sure into which category my story fits, but I do know it still hurts, years later.

Having a crush on someone is like putting your heart in a Ziploc bag and checking it at the airport luggage counter. There is a chance it will make the trip and come out unscathed, but there is a much greater chance that it will be bruised in some way.

Check "Yes" or "No," But Don't Check "No"

Did you ever send or receive one of those notes in junior high? Usually they came in the form of a folded piece of notebook paper that read, "I like you. Do you like me? Check yes or no." Now that I think back on it, I hope I received more than I sent!

Sometimes as we get older and relationships become more complicated, we want to go back to that simple system.

One thing I learned from my experience in junior high is that checking "no" *is* an option. It is altogether possible that the object of our desire does not esteem us as the object of his or her desire. How devastating! A true crush means that we have admired, thought about, studied, and dreamed about someone. Yet, quite often, the desired relationship does not ever materialize. When the window of hope is shut in our face, it can be quite painful. The person that we have built all our plans around is suddenly gone, and it is as if a trap door was opened beneath our feet.

Sometimes we lose our crush because we are honest about our feelings and the object of our affections does not reciprocate them. We can also lose our crush if that person finds someone else in whom he or she is interested. Or circumstances may prevent us from getting together: one person moves away, parents won't allow one of us to date, or one or both of us feel like God is somehow saying "No," or "Wait." In all of these cases the blow is crushing. As in any disappointing situation, it is good to talk to someone about how you are feeling. Journaling is great, too, because you have the freedom to express any thoughts you want without worrying about the information getting out to those whom you don't want to know about it.

"This Too Shall Pass"

Although your crush and your feelings are as big as the world to you when they happen, it is important to realize that as time passes, so will these experiences. Maybe you are embarrassed that your crush found out how you felt, or hurt that he or she chose someone else. You will get past these feelings soon enough. Squint your eyes and try your best to look through your feelings to the other side of your experience. Look for a place where you will be happy and content without any girl or guy, or picture yourself in a healthy relationship with someone who treats you as well as you deserve to be treated; a relationship that comes about in God's good timing. In one of my favorite books, *Don't Sweat the Small Stuff for Teens*, Richard Carlson speaks about the passing of time and our feelings.

> You can take great comfort in knowing that everything passes. Since there are no exceptions—none—it means that if you are sad, you won't always be sad. If you fail, you'll bounce back. If someone hurt you, that feeling will change. If you lose a love, there will be another. Indeed, there is something very reassuring in knowing that, whatever it is, however hard it seems, it too will pass.[1]

If it is in your heart to be in a relationship, know that God has put that desire in your heart for a reason and that he will fulfill it when the time is right. Perhaps right now you simply need to be focused on school, family, friendships, and your relationship with God, as well as on knowing yourself. When the right relationship is meant to happen, it will. You can't prevent God from bringing you good things any more than you can manipulate him into giving you relationships and blessings you are not meant to have yet. "'For I know the plans I have for you,' declares the Lord, 'plans to prosper you and not to harm you, plans to give you hope and a future'" (Jer 29:11).

Think About It

Since crushes affect all of us at one time or another, and we are disappointed by many of them, here are a couple of things to consider.

Sibling Factor

The apostle Peter wrote, "Honor all men. Love the brotherhood" (1 Pt 2:17a, KJV). Think about what this means. If you have asked Christ to forgive you of your sin and come into your life, you have become part of the family of God. When you are attracted to another Christian, remember that he or she is also your brother or sister in Christ. We are to honor one another in all we say and do.

If you have an earthly sister, you should love her unselfishly. You should want what is best for her, no matter what you want. Now, let's apply that principle to a crush. If we have a crush on someone who is our brother or sister in Christ, we should also want what is best for that person. Sometimes what is best for that person—and for us, for that matter—is not what we want.

Amy, one of my best friends in high school, was totally obsessed with a boy named Matt. If she had a class with him, she would sit near him and watch his every move. She would ask other people questions about him and try to get closer to his friends. She even collected pictures of him. Amy was a great friend to me, but she had a slightly wrong perspective on Matt.

One day, we heard that Matt had asked out a nice girl from another class. Amy was totally devastated. All of her work and all of her hope was for nothing. She was angry with Matt and swore to break up his relationship with his new girlfriend at all costs.

Amy had a selfish desire for Matt. She wanted him, no matter what. She had not even considered what was best for Matt. She thought she was showing love toward Matt, but she wanted what she thought was best for her, not what was best for him.

As hard as it is, we need to change our perspective when a situation like this occurs. Have you ever ordered dessert at a restaurant only to have the waiter tell you that they are out of the dessert you ordered? When this happens I usually choose something else. Every now and then, the dessert I receive is better than the one I originally ordered. When a crush gets away, you have an opportunity to create a better life than what you ordered. It is difficult to keep the right perspective, but with God's help you'll eventually be able to smile when you see the new couple walk by.

Valerie, one of my best friends at college, had her eye on a boy named Kevin. She had been friends with him for over a year and truly appreciated Kevin's relationship with God. She could have easily become obsessed about him, but she did not allow herself to do so. She treated him as a beloved brother. When he needed help on a school project, she eagerly volunteered. She loved him unselfishly, even when there was no hint of a romantic relationship on the horizon. One day, for no specific reason, Kevin realized how awesome Valerie is. He soon asked her out and they enjoyed a great relationship. Yet Valerie's genuine affection for him did not depend on her hopes of a dating relationship coming true.

There is a difference in how we can choose to treat our crushes. We can view them selfishly, as objects of our desire, or we can view them as brothers or sisters we should care for and serve unselfishly.

Who's on First?

There was another difference between how Amy and Valerie dealt with their crushes. Amy left God out of the picture; Valerie clung to God even more closely during this time. The psalmist gives us good advice for this situation: "My soul finds rest in God alone; my salvation comes from him" (Ps 62:1). God must remain our focus, no matter what the storm or what the distraction. When our attraction and appreciation turn into obsession and selfish desire, we make it virtually impossible for God to bless us in any way.

I believe that God loves us so much he does not want us to leave his side. When I think about that, I picture a three-year-old child clinging to her father's leg. Crushes can either lead us away from our Father or keep us right beside him. We have to decide which it will be. Maybe one day that three-year-old child will peek around her Father's leg to see a little boy clinging to the other leg. Or perhaps not. Yet if she allows her Father to meet her need for love, she will be happy either way.

"He [God] alone is my rock and my salvation; he is my fortress, I will not be shaken. My salvation and my honor depend on God; he is my mighty rock, my refuge" (Ps 62:6-7).

While we wait for the day when we find someone with whom to serve God, we need to remember that God himself is enough.

Prayer Starters

What is the hardest part of having a crush on someone?

_____

_____

_____

When you talk to God about your crush, how do you feel?

_____

_____

What do you think God has been teaching you through this experience?

_____

_____

_____

_____

Scripture Assignment
Psalm 33:18; Psalm 73:23

A Prayer for When You Are Crushed by a Crush

Dear Father of my spirit,

I know that having a crush isn't a big deal to many people, but it is a big deal to me. I just like _____ so much, that I cannot quit thinking about _____ [him or her]. I don't know if _____ will ever like me, but help me remember that you want the best for me. I have to keep the right perspective on this situation and keep in mind that I don't need anyone but you to be happy. Father, help me keep my feelings in check and keep you first in my life. Be with me as I deal with this crushing crush.

In your name,

Amen

ELEVEN

When You Go Through a Breakup

He was the best friend I ever had. We had known each other for six years, watching each other grow and change and keeping up with each other's lives during our nightly phone conversations. We had tried to date several times before, with little success. I never seemed to stay interested in him. Finally, in his senior year of high school and my junior year, I made a resolute decision that I really wanted to date him. I knew he was chasing a gorgeous girl from another school and I was losing him. I wanted to be the girl on his arm.

Brent was the kind of goofy guy who always ended up with his foot in his mouth, but he had the most compassionate heart. He also had deep blue eyes that made me melt time and time again. I was confident that once I told him how I felt and what I had decided, he would forget the blonde he was chasing and fall madly in love with me. When he asked me to his senior prom I decided that was *the* night to tell him.

After the prom, before he took me home, I told him that we needed to talk. He responded with a dumbfounded "OK." I had practiced my speech for weeks, but all my emotions came rushing out completely uncontrolled. Tears were mixed with hope. As I sat across from him in the car, I simply offered him my heart.

He slowly sighed and I saw a tear slide down his cheek. I had thought that after my speech he would sweep me up into his arms and we would live happily ever after, but apparently no one had told him how the story was supposed to end. Without a word he gave me a half-hearted hug and started the engine. Before we pulled out he calmly stared straight out of the windshield and said, "I can't be with you, Britt." He did not want me, not anymore.

When your heart is broken it can seem as though the world has stopped moving. Every memory from your past relationship is a vivid scene in your mind. You look around and see elderly couples, middle-aged couples, and young couples— couples everywhere! Their happiness seems to you like a slap in the face. You feel sick every time you see a romantic couple holding hands. Treasured cards, letters, pictures, and dried flowers seem to pour out of every drawer and corner of your home, reminding you of a time when your relationship was full of possibility. Your mind becomes a broken record of past events and conversations. Deep inside your spirit an ugly monster called "regret" is born.

Most of us have gone through this at some point in our lives. Heartbreak is a paradox because it makes you feel all alone in this big, cruel world, yet millions of others are experiencing pain like yours at the same time. How do you truly start the healing process? Is there hope? It may not feel like it at the time, but I promise you there is!

Take Out the Trash

Everyone loves a good party. When the right kind of music, people, and food are there, it seems as though no one has a care in the world. Everything is just plain fun. Yet, as you know if you have ever hosted a party, it's depressing after your last guest leaves to turn and look at what is left. Empty soda cans sit by empty chairs. The living room is so destroyed that your dog cannot find a place to lie down. There is trash everywhere, and inevitably someone has forgotten his or her coat. It is absolutely disheartening.

That's what it feels like at the end of a relationship. It was a blast while it lasted, but when it is over there are fragmented emotions everywhere and a deep depression settles in. The fun has come to an end. Usually someone (maybe you?) has left part of his or her heart behind. At this point it's important to realize that it is OK to be sorrowful. There will be a grieving process much like you would endure if a loved one passed away.

Every party host knows that the cleaning up process has to begin somewhere, so let's talk about taking out the trash. There are three ways to get rid of the trash that a broken heart has left:

1. Turn to God
2. Trap it in a journal
3. Trash talk with a friend

Turn to God

I can say without a doubt that every time I have gone through heartbreak there was something that God wanted to teach me about himself. If you look for it, you will find a lesson in your heartache, too.

Talk to God, out loud if you can. This helps you to view

prayer as a conversation. I do not advocate doing this in the middle of the mall or at a library, but you can usually find a secluded spot to speak to God. If home is not an option, try your car, or talk to him at the bus stop. (Again, this works best if you're alone.) Tell him exactly how you feel. Even cry to him. Do not leave anything out. God cares about even the smallest details of our lives. Matthew 10:29-31 says, "Are not two sparrows sold for a penny? Yet not one of them will fall to the ground apart from the will of your Father. And even the very hairs of your head are all numbered. So don't be afraid; you are worth more than many sparrows."

God is never going to waste your pain. Dick Innes teaches this principle in his book *How to Mend a Broken Heart*.

Remember it is one thing to hurt. It is another thing to allow your pain to hurt you. Accept your hurt as an opportunity to heal, to grow, and to become a more understanding, sensitive, compassionate, and creative person. It has been costly. Don't waste it. Invest it wisely in your own growth and in the enrichment of other people's lives as well.[1]

The Bible is full of wisdom and great teaching for us, but it's often hard to know where to start. The Book of Psalms is excellent reading for the brokenhearted. King David experienced pain greater than most of us will ever have to face. He records this in many different psalms. One of my favorites is Psalm 77. "I cried out to God for help; I cried out to God to hear me. When I was in distress, I sought the Lord; at night I stretched out untiring hands and my soul refused to be comforted" (Ps 77:1-2).

I take comfort in realizing that God thought David's hurts were important enough to include in his letter to his children, the Bible. God knows we hurt. He created our emotions and feelings. Jesus himself was 100 percent man as well as 100 percent God. Think of how he felt when his best friends, the disciples, deserted him. Think of his heartbreak when his heavenly Father had to forsake him while Jesus carried our sins on the cross. God completely understands our pain. Humans will always disappoint us, but, praise God, Jesus will not.

Trap It in a Journal
It has been proven that writing down our thoughts and feelings has a therapeutic effect. I am sold on this concept. I have been a "journaling freak" for six years. This may not seem like an extremely long time, but it's almost a third of my life—long enough for me to see the benefits it has to offer.

I also combine prayer with my journaling. I do not write, "Dear Diary." I write, "Dear God." Writing out your prayers is another thing you can do, besides praying silently, if you cannot otherwise get alone with God to speak to him. You will be amazed as you look back on your entries from years past and see how God's miracles have unfolded in your life. You do not have to write only prayers. You can record any feelings or thoughts. If your ex-girlfriend or ex-boyfriend has made you angry, write her or him a letter in your journal. You do not have to deliver it. (In many cases, it's better if you don't.) Yet you'll still reap the benefits of going through the process.

Trash Talk With Someone

"Trash talking" often refers to saying bad things about some-one or something. In this case, however, I'm talking about disposing of the emotional trash in your life by talking it out with a close friend—someone who will support you in your hurt and confusion.

This is pretty straightforward advice, but there are some things to consider when choosing someone to whom you will pour out your heart. First of all, do not pick someone who is going to run back to the person who broke your heart and tell him or her everything you said. You need a person who will listen and not repeat your thoughts and feelings.

Choose someone who is safe. Often, our close relationships are interconnected. Be sure you don't talk with someone who is related to your "ex"—or worse, someone who has a crush on him or her. What you need right now is someone impartial who will support you and not use the information you give him or her—either accidentally or on purpose.

Make sure that your friend also has faith in Jesus Christ. Second Corinthians 6:14 says, "For what do righteousness and wickedness have in common? Or what fellowship can light have with darkness?" If your friend does not share your faith, then any advice he or she gives may be off center. A Christian friend can help you discover what God is teaching you through your pain.

Finally, choose someone whose life is stable. When our hearts are broken we tend to flock to others who are going through similar pain. Try not to do this. Friends who are in pain have their own issues they may need to deal with before they can sit down and rationally help you work through yours.

Someone with all these qualities is a good choice. Do not forget that your pastor or a Christian counselor is a good choice as well. Many Christian colleges and universities also offer free counseling. Do not be afraid to take advantage of the resources available to you.

Moving Forward, Moving On

You will have one of two feelings at this point. Either you do not want to move on emotionally from the person who hurt you or you do indeed want to move on. If you do not want to move on, that feeling is OK. Moving on will take time, and it is natural to want to hang on to a relationship that has been dear to you. Remember, if you have gone through a breakup, God can and will use your experience for good. Thankfully, you cannot live in this place of sadness forever. Your only choice is to eventually move forward. Again Dick Innes advises in his book *How to Mend a Broken Heart,* "Life can only be understood by looking backward, but it must be lived by looking forward."[2] You may not be ready now, but you will be one day. In the meantime, go ahead and read the following section with an open mind.

If, on the other hand, you do want to move on, congratulations! The battle is half won. Here are some tips to help you succeed.

Don't Set Yourself Up to Lose

I have seen many friends go through heart-wrenching breakups only to sabotage any hope of truly moving on. There are certain behaviors and actions that are simply going to increase your chances of failing.

One such behavior is listening to depressing music. Everyone has heard the joke, "What do you get when you play a country song backward?" Answer: "You get your house, your wife, and your dog back." Be it country, pop, or any other kind of music we listen to, we need to be especially careful when we are recovering from a breakup. Imagine going through a painful heartbreak while listening to any kind of depressing music. You will do yourself no good. Try to avoid any kind of music that is not uplifting until you are over your broken relationship. Yes, this does include listening to "your song" over and over again.

Surroundings also matter. If your room is plastered with Johnny's pictures and Johnny's letters, then Johnny is not going anywhere. And you are definitely not moving on from him. No one is advocating a bonfire of Johnny paraphernalia, but you can easily put those photos, ticket stubs, and dried flowers in your closet or in a shoebox. Maybe someday you'll be ready to fondly paste them in a scrapbook. Or maybe you'll pitch them in the garbage. For now, just put them away where you don't have to deal with them until you're emotionally ready. Out of sight, out of mind. (No cheating and peeking. If you can't let go, give them to a friend or parent for safekeeping.)

The summer before college, a good friend of mine broke up with a girl he had been dating for almost a year. They broke up because she had cheated on him with at least two other guys. The odd thing was that although they broke up they never quit calling one another. I do not mean that they spoke occasionally; I mean that they called each other at least once a day. Needless to say, they got back together, broke up again, and the vicious cycle continued. If you break up with someone, separate yourself from him or her until you are over it. A scar will not heal if you keep opening up the wound.

Another important thing is to resist the temptation to feel worthless or unimportant if your girlfriend or boyfriend broke up with you. Think about it. Everyone can find a relationship if they lower their standards enough. If you lower your standards you certainly will find another person to date, but you will suffer the consequences of pairing off with someone who is not good for you. Imagine being romantically involved with someone who drinks or does drugs, who does not share your faith, or who pressures you sexually. All of these options are much worse than being on your own for a time. Being single does not mean you are not good enough for a date, it means that God has not yet sent the *right* person your way.

Do Equip Yourself to Win

So you are single again, huh? Great! Now you can focus on growing, both spiritually and emotionally, and on taking care of yourself physically. Those things are much harder to do when you are committed and responsible to another person. Right now, you can grow in the Lord and dedicate all the time you need to daily devotions. You can observe what areas of life you need to mature in and start working on them. You can get back to that exercise program you quit because you never had time. Nothing makes you feel better after having your heart broken than getting in shape and looking and feeling good inside and out!

These are some ways to focus on yourself when preparing to win, but a huge part of succeeding in life is putting others first by serving them. After my boyfriend Craig and I broke up, I began a ministry to the elderly. After Brent and I broke up, I started volunteering at a Christian TV station. After Nick and I broke up in college, I started writing this book. All of these projects helped me work through my loneliness and get involved in ministry. Use your time alone to serve God by serving the people around you.

Father Knows Best

Have you ever had insomnia and found yourself watching "Nick at Nite" in the early morning hours? If so, you probably have caught reruns of an old TV show called "Father Knows Best." The show is much like other sitcoms of that era. What is unique about it is that the show revolved around a father's response to his children's decisions. The father gave his children advice that always turned out to be the best plan of action. God is your Father, and, believe it or not, he does know best.

Brent did end up with the gorgeous blonde he was chasing and I did lose him as a best friend. It was one of the hardest times in my life. I would cry myself to sleep and wake up and cry again. His letters and notes were strewn about my room, reminding me of him. I did a lot of praying and a lot of journaling during that time. God was the only one who knew exactly what was going on with me, and he was the only one who got me through it.

One bright Saturday I heard a car horn sound from my driveway. I peeked out the window and saw Brent in a brand-new Camaro convertible. I felt a smile spread across my face as I ran out to meet him. I had not seen him or talked to him in several months. He was happy to see me, but something was wrong. "Can I tell you something, Britt?" Of course he could! We told each other everything, or at least we used to. I could tell that he was scared to tell me.

After pausing for a long time he quietly said, "I have been drinking a lot in the past few months." I was disappointed that this great guy had chosen a wrong path, but I could see in his eyes the shame he felt. He had come to me to ask for help. Suddenly it hit me. I might have been dating him through all of this! I might have been tempted to drink, too. Only months earlier, I had prayed for God to let me be with Brent, but God said "No." It was hard to understand why at the time. You may be wondering "why" in your situation. Believe it or not, God knows what he is doing. He is all-knowing and all-powerful. He could have answered "Yes" to my prayers to be with Brent, but he knew where Brent was headed and he loved me enough to protect me from that situation. Thank you, Lord. Father really does know best.

Prayer Starters

How has this breakup affected how you view your life?

_____

_____

_____

_____

_____

_____

What do you think God may be teaching you through this time in your life?

_____

_____

_____

_____

_____

What consequences might this breakup have protected you from?

_____

_____

_____

_____

_____

_____

Scripture Assignment
Psalm 34:17-22

A Prayer for When You Go Through a Breakup

Father God,

I come before you feeling very incomplete. I cannot remember a breakup ever affecting me this deeply. My thoughts are filled with _____. I cannot seem to escape it. Everywhere I turn something reminds me of our relationship and the memories we shared. It feels like I am in a prison, no matter where I go. I know that eventually I will get over this breakup, but right now the pain is almost unbearable. Please be with me here in my time of sorrow. Give me work to do for you so that I will work through my loneliness. Bring family and friends into my life so that I can stay close to my loved ones. Protect me from bitterness and gossip. I am so easily tempted in my pain and anger. Help me to keep you first in my mind. I must remember that you can do something beautiful with my pain.

In your strength,

Amen

TWELVE

When You've Made a Mistake

Haley and I attended different high schools but we had many mutual friends. She had a wonderful sense of humor. No matter how my day had gone, when I called her I began to smile.

However, although Haley was an amazing girl with many gifts and talents, she did not get a lot of attention from boys. When she did receive attention she didn't really know how to respond. Often she would brag about the attention as if to prove that someone was interested in her.

One day on a trip to the mall, Haley announced to me and a few other friends that she had found a new "love of her life." He was two years older than she and he went to her high school, so we didn't know too much about him.

I did not pry into her relationship but soon learned that this guy was not a Christian. I knew that this would cause problems for her. The Bible tells us not to be "unequally yoked" with unbelievers (2 Cor 6:14). That doesn't mean we shouldn't be friends with them; it means that we should not make them the closest, most intimate allies in our lives.

In biblical times, when oxen drew a cart they were yoked together in their work. If one was bigger than the other, they could not pull the cart evenly. It might even break! In the same way, if we commit ourselves in relationships with those who don't love God we jeopardize our ability to do our job, which is listening to God's voice and living out the wonderful lives he has in store for us.

Unfortunately, dating a non-Christian did cause problems for Haley. Rumors soon began to fly in our circle of friends about this guy. Eventually, I heard through the grapevine that she had slept with him. The next week, Haley told me the story herself, her eyes swollen from crying. In the months to follow, Haley was filled with guilt and regret. Soon she and her boyfriend broke up, which intensified the hurt.

Once Haley's mistake was made (dating a nonbeliever), she had another decision to make: she could either turn from her wrong choice or give up her convictions and continue living the way she wanted. Unfortunately, Haley chose the latter. She was so afraid that no guy would want her unless she acted a certain way that she gave in to temptation.

Perhaps you relate to Haley's mistakes. Or perhaps you have made other mistakes in your life. I know I have! The point is, we all make bad choices and we all have to deal with the aftermath. We wrestle with guilt, with our anger toward ourselves, with hopelessness, and with accepting God's forgiveness. Every emotion becomes mixed in with the rest, like a bunch of necklaces knotted up in a drawer. Every road we might take seems wrong. Everywhere we look, everyone seems to be judging us.

When Decisions Go Bad

You and I aren't alone in making bad choices. Moses, the chosen leader of God's people, killed an Egyptian before leading God's people out of Egypt. King David, ruler of God's people, committed adultery with Bathsheba and ordered her husband's death. Peter, a chosen disciple of Jesus Christ, three times denied knowing him. Clearly, even the Bible's most acclaimed heroes made very bad decisions at some points in their lives. Everyone makes mistakes: sometimes big ones, sometimes small. The Bible tells us over and over again that we are *all* sinful creatures. "For all have sinned and come short of the glory of God" (Rom 3:23, KJV).

I am not saying that we have a right to do wrong because everyone else does. I am saying that mistakes come with the territory of being human. We all need to realize we are not the only ones who have committed a certain sin. Sin and the regret that naturally accompanies it are common to mankind, but the reactions to sin are varied. Each of us must choose how to respond to our regret. Erwin Lutzer, in *Managing Your Emotions*, says, "The regret will not change what has happened in the past, but it can lead to future changes. God can still use that emotion of regret to make the best of the future."[1]

No Mistake Is Too Big for God to Forgive

Becoming a Christian is like entering a maze, with numerous paths from which to choose. You live your life one way or another. You cannot take more than one path in the maze at once, nor can you live out your life both in obedience to God and according to your own selfish desires.

Sometimes you run into a dead end in life because you have made a bad decision. Because of where you have ended up, you feel a great amount of remorse for your decision. When this happens, you can decide whether to stay in the dead end, regretting the past, or turn around and search for the right passageway.

Sometimes we get stuck in a dead end because we cannot imagine God would forgive us of so great a sin. God has included numerous verses in the Bible to reassure us of his forgiveness of even the greatest mistakes. One of my favorite verses is found in Isaiah. "I have swept away your offenses like a cloud, your sins like the morning mist. Return to me, for I have redeemed you" (Is 44:22). Drugs? Alcohol? Premarital sex? Betrayal of a friend? Cheating? Lying? Running away? Something worse? Believe it or not, there is no mistake bigger than God's forgiveness. It is impossible for us to commit sins so great or so many that God will not take us back if we go to him in true repentance, seeking to change our ways. This knowledge should not give us license to sin; it should spur us on to serve him even more faithfully because of his mercy.

What must we do to turn from our sins and seek God's forgiveness? The Bible says, "If we confess our sins, he is faithful and just to forgive us our sins and to cleanse us from all unrighteousness" (1 Jn 1:9, KJV). Did you catch that "if"? We must confess our sin before we can be forgiven. Confessing means admitting your wrongdoing before the Lord in a spirit of remorse. Confessing means telling God that you made a mistake and that you are truly sorry. The Bible tells us that when we confess, he is faithful and just and *will* forgive us of our sin. Peace is found in confession. In Psalm 32, David described the suffering that led to his confession.

When I kept silent about my sin, my body wasted away through my groaning all day long. For day and night thy hand was heavy upon me; my vitality was drained away as with the fever heat of the summer. I acknowledged my sin to thee, and my iniquity I did not hide; I said, "I will confess my transgressions to the Lord;" and thou didst forgive the guilt of my sin.

PSALM 32:3-5, NASB

David explains the pain that he had before he confessed his sin to God. His unconfessed sin even affected him physically. His regret consumed him until he asked for God's forgiveness. Confessing means bringing before God the sinful disobedience of our hearts and minds. It means that we not only acknowledge our sinful behavior, we also turn from it. True confession comes hand in hand with a change of heart.

Accepting the Consequences

I remember talking back to my mother when I was little and being sorry afterward for what I had done. I would try to talk my father out of my punishment using the logic that I was already sorry. I don't think it worked even one time. My parents did not let me off the hook because they had to teach me that there are always consequences for our actions.

When we make a mistake, no matter what the condition of our heart, the consequences will follow. Perhaps the consequence is a pregnancy or a disease. The consequence might be a lost friendship or something as severe as jail time. Facing the hardships that mistakes bring may take us into a very cold and lonely time. Yet know that in your darkest hour God is right beside you, keeping you in his focus. "He found him in a desert land, and in the waste howling wilderness; he led him about, he instructed him, he kept him as the apple of his eye" (Dt 32:10, KJV). That verse is a part of the Song of Moses, which Moses taught the Israelites, hoping to strengthen their faith.

Try reading that verse again, filling in your name:

"He [God] found _____ in a desert land, and in the waste howling wilderness; he led _____ about, he instructed _____, he kept _____ as the apple of his eye."

That's how much God loves you. Whatever desert land (or consequences of sin) you find yourself in, God is there with you.

Moses himself had to deal with the consequences of his actions. God didn't let even him off the hook! The Bible tells us in Numbers 20 that the Israelites were complaining because they had no water for themselves and for their livestock. At this time they were in the wilderness, waiting on God to give them the Promised Land. The Lord heard the people's cries and instructed Moses to speak to a rock so that it would bring forth water for the people. Instead of following God's instructions, Moses struck the rock two times with his rod. We don't know why. Maybe Moses thought he could "help along" God's miracle by physically shaking up the rock. In any case, he wasn't obedient. Thankfully, God, in his mercy, allowed water to come forth anyway, but because of Moses' disobedience the Lord told him that he would not lead the people into the Promised Land (see Nm 20:12). Somebody else got that honor, and Moses missed out on one of the biggest blessings he was meant to receive.

What we can learn from all of this is that there were consequences to Moses' actions (he missed out on a really cool blessing), but one mistake did not ruin his life. Moses is listed in Hebrews 11 among the heroes of the faith. He was still considered a role model, though he made several mistakes. God can still use you and me, too, no matter what mistakes we have made in the past.

The People Factor

I love to ski. I have been skiing only a handful of times, but I really enjoy it. However, I think I maybe could get into the *Guinness Book of World Records* for the greatest number of falls in one day. My favorite thing about skiing is the bunny hill. (Please hold your laughter.) It is smooth and calm, and there are very few ways to injure yourself on that hill.

One of the bunny hills I have skied is on Sugar Mountain in North Carolina. At the bottom of the hill is a rope-tow instead of a chairlift. The way it works is quite simple: You line your skis up and hold on to this rope as it pulls you to the top. The tricky thing about the rope-tow is that if you fall while it is pulling you up the mountain, all of the people behind you fall, because the rope keeps going, whether you do or not. I made this happen several times. As you can imagine, I wasn't too popular with my fellow skiers that day.

One of the hardest things about making a big mistake is the number of other people it affects. Think about everyone who looks up to you. There are probably more than you realize. There are your brothers and sisters, your cousins, the neighbors and friends of yours who are younger Christians, other classmates. All of these people are looking up to you as an example. They are like the people following you up that mountain on the rope-tow. If you fall, they might fall, too.

Sin does not affect only us. Yet we shouldn't let this discourage us. It is just as easy to grab on to the rope as it is to let go. So hang on—even when times get rough. Very soon, you'll be trucking up that mountain again with who knows how many people following your lead.

Keeping on Track

A while ago a very good friend of mine strayed from his commitment to Christ. He wanted to do his own thing in life, while giving little thought to how God felt about it. I sat down and had a long discussion with him because I cared so much for him. He talked with me as if we were on two different planets: mine, a planet where you try to please God, and his, a planet where you get to do whatever you want. I could see in his eyes that he felt we had little in common. Maybe he felt like he had made too many mistakes to ever go back to where he was before.

I reminded him that there is only one small difference between serving God and serving yourself, only one thing separating those two planets. The difference is a decision. Every minute you must decide whom you will serve, whom you will try to please.

We have all chosen to please ourselves over God at some

time in our lives, but don't let your regret and your guilt keep you from making the right decision now and in the future. You may have a bunch of poor decisions in your past. Yet you have a lifetime of new opportunities ahead.

Prayer Starters

Which of your mistakes bothers you the most right now?

_____

_____

_____

_____

How has your mistake made you feel?

_____

_____

_____

_____

Have you confessed your mistake to God?

_____

_____

_____

_____

What has God taught you through your mistake?

_____

_____

_____

Scripture Assignment
Psalm 71

A Prayer for When You've Made a Mistake

Gracious Redeemer,

I have fallen on my face before you. I made a bad decision, which has affected my relationship with you and others. With each breath I take in more guilt. I can't seem to get rid of it. I am so sorry for _____. I don't want to give you excuses or explanations. I just want to humbly ask you for forgiveness. Thank you for your promise in 1 John 1:9 to forgive our confessed sin. I ask you for help in overcoming this temptation in the future. Thank you for always loving me, no matter what mistakes I make.

In your loving name,

Amen

THIRTEEN

When You Have to Make a Decision

It was coming down to the wire. I had to choose. Most of my high school friends had already made their decisions. No, it wasn't the most important decision of my life, but it was a very important one: I had to decide where I was going to go to college.

Choosing a college is a decision that can affect so many things: Who some lifelong friends will be, meeting a potential spouse, and developing personal interests and career options. Especially important is receiving the type of education that will further goals and dreams.

It was the summer before my senior year of high school and I was torn between two strong Christian colleges, both of which had accepted me. Money was a huge factor. One school was closer, cheaper, and had offered me a scholarship, but that was the one I liked the least. It was a good school, but Cedarville had a technological edge. I began to pray specifically that God would give me guidance by August.

During the summer, my grandfather began to suffer from some minor health problems. No one in my family was overly concerned, least of all me. My grandpa was more athletic than I! He ate right, exercised, and took vitamins. I felt certain that, given a choice, our nation's army would choose him at age seventy over legions of strong eighteen-year-olds. There was no way my grandpa was sick.

However, Grandpa began to eat less and have less energy. After weeks of deterioration, he flew from Florida to my home in North Carolina to see a specialist. After three weeks of tests, he was diagnosed with stomach cancer—the same type of cancer that had taken the lives of his father and brother. My mother knew the impact of this diagnosis. However, I did not. I was sure he would make it. He was my grandpa.

In my last conversation alone with him, out of the blue he said, "Britt, I want you to look into that Cedarville school."

"OK, Grandpa," I said. "I've been accepted and I'll definitely think about it."

"If you didn't like it you wouldn't have to stay." Just then a nurse came in to get him for surgery. But before the nurse took him away he looked at me and said, "It is a good school, sweetheart, but you can make it better."

As she wheeled him away, the weight of his words began to hit me. I had faith in the surgery. I didn't doubt his full recovery at all. Yet I was surprised that Grandpa had chosen that moment, of all times, to talk to me about choosing a college.

My grandfather lost his battle with cancer on July 31, 1998. It was one day before the first of August, the date by which I had asked God to direct me to the school that was right for me.

Decisions can be excruciating. As teens and young adults, we strive to please our parents, our relatives, our friends, our teachers, and God with our choices. It is hard—if not impossible—to keep everyone happy. Tough decisions can be exasperating or frustrating due to their difficulty. It is often easier to avoid the responsibility and let someone else decide for us. In my case, I could have asked my parents to make my decision for me. Or I could have held off on making a decision until one of the schools assumed I wasn't coming. Yet being passive wouldn't have been in my best interest. Nor would it have brought me any closer to my God. It is important and helpful for us to remember that each decision is an appointment—a chance for us to find God's will and embrace it.

Five S's of Tough Decision-Making

Decisions will always be tough, but there are keys to helping us make good decisions. I have broken them down into the five S's of decision making.

Solicit Advice

Proverbs 24:6 says, "For by wise counsel shalt thou make war, and in a multitude of counselors there is safety" (KJV). You and I might not be going off to battle in a true military sense. Yet the struggles of life often feel like a type of war, and we can benefit a lot from the wisdom of the people we love and trust.

Think of all the people around you at school, at church, in your neighborhood, and in your family. All have had unique experiences that have taught them a great deal. If your loved ones are given an opportunity to share the wisdom they have gained through hard times, then in a very real way, their pain was worth it. You can enrich the lives of those people, young or old, by giving them an opportunity to share the lessons God has taught them. You can also benefit from their wisdom.

Of course, you will find that advice given concerning your decision will vary from person to person. However, if you are asking godly Christians for advice, you are certain to gain from their collective wisdom insights that will help you in making your own choice. If you are rooted in a solid Christian church, consider asking one or all of the pastors for their advice. Ask your Sunday school teacher or youth leader as well.

In addition to these sources, do not overlook the authority figures in your life. If you are like most teens, you probably do not enjoy the lectures given by your parents. Yet why not shock them and ask for their input *before* they lecture you? Believe it or not, your parents do know you better than anyone else does, and they can give you more insight into your decisions than you realize.

Whether friends or family, leaders or mentors, the advice of God's people will give you the guidance you want and need to make your tough decisions.

Seal It With Prayer

Of course, not every decision requires the asking of God's advice. You probably can decide on your own what you want to watch on TV tonight or what toppings to order when you call in your order for pizza. When it comes to the important decisions in life, though, you and I need all the help we can get—especially help that comes from the One who always knows what is best for us.

Every step of your decision-making process can be covered with prayer. Pray that God will show you his will clearly so that you can please him with your decision. When you pray, make sure that you are submitting to God's will and not simply seeking your own. God doesn't always give us answers all at once.

Sometimes he just tells us what to do next.

The important thing to remember is to be patient and trust God even when he seems silent.

Study Scripture

When I was younger and I needed to figure something out, I would sometimes adhere to the "flip and stick" method of finding God's will. That's when you flip through your Bible and, without looking, stick your finger somewhere on a page to see if God will give you a specific verse that will direct you in your situation. After reading about fifty verses this way, I found one or two that did relate to my specific situation. However, that method is not exactly what I mean by studying Scripture to seek God's will.

First of all, if one option you are considering requires breaking any of God's commands, like lying or stealing—or even being dishonest or unkind—then you know right away that it is not God's will. Even if your motivation feels right, breaking God's rules is always wrong. This simple test will rule out more options than you would expect!

Next, look for passages in the Bible that might help you in your situation. In the back of most Bibles is a concordance, which you can use to help you search out your questions. Look up a key word, like "wisdom." The concordance will give you a list of all of the passages that include that word. Your Bible may have only a small concordance, or may not have one at all, in which case you can look for a larger concordance in your local library or Christian bookstore. If looking for a key word doesn't help, you can perhaps look in a topical Bible for answers to your question. Those types of Bibles can also be found in your local bookstore or library.

Unfortunately, God does not tell us in Scripture specifically what to do in every given situation. He did, however write one comprehensive book, the Bible, that contains all the general guidance we need for whatever we encounter in our lives. The more you read Scripture, the more that guidance will be available to you, imbedded in your mind and spirit, when you need it.

Search for Personal Desires and Feelings

Emotions often get a bad rap when it comes to making choices. They are sometimes portrayed as misleading, but it is important to consider your own desires and feelings when making decisions. Psalm 37 says, "Delight thyself also in the Lord; and he shall give thee the desires of thine heart" (Ps 37:4, KJV). This does not mean that if we desire to have a closet full of Gap clothing, God will give it to us. It does mean that if our hearts are right with God and we delight in him, then our desires will be his desires. Those desires are often a good indicator of what we should choose in a given situation.

If I go into an ice cream shop, I have to decide which of the delicious flavors to eat. I may ask the employee to let me taste the cookie dough ice cream and the mint chocolate chip ice cream. The cookie dough hits the spot, but the mint chocolate chip doesn't even taste good to me. If I don't like one of these flavors, my decision just got a lot easier. "I will take a scoop of cookie dough in a sugar cone, please."

In this same way, your personal preferences and desires play an important role in helping you to determine God's will. If you have two job offers and you totally dislike one of them, then you have a big clue as to where you should be going. Unless we want to go against God's Word, or unless God has something better in store for us, God does not work against our desires. However, our desires should not be the sole basis for a decision.

Seek Opened and Closed Doors
The last step in the decision-making process is searching for opened and closed doors. What we are doing here is looking for a green light (or red light) from God.

A couple of years ago, my family and I took a vacation to Myrtle Beach, South Carolina, with my aunt and uncle. After several days, we were running out of things to do, so we picked up a brochure on a place called Maze Mania. This tourist trap is a very large maze, whose walls are made of wooden planks reaching nine feet in height. Adults and kids race through the maze in an attempt to beat the clock and win a prize. My uncle, my cousin, my father, and I accepted the challenge.

When we arrived, we saw that the best time was four minutes. I was determined to beat that record. The people operating the attraction opened the door to the colorful maze and yelled, "Go!" The four of us started out together but soon split up in the many rooms, hallways, and alleys. I could see as I was winding my way around that the operators could change the configuration of the maze by opening and closing doors to different passageways.

The day we ran the maze, the temperature was at least ninety degrees. There was no shade in the maze and nowhere to sit down. I kept trying hallway after hallway, but I always ended up back where I began. I ran into my cousin once, who, in frustration, was trying unsuccessfully to climb the nine-foot wall. Another time, I ran into my father, who was absolutely convinced that my uncle had found his way out and shut one of the doors on us for a joke.

Suddenly, Dad and I had a brainstorm. We would leave tiny pieces of paper on the ground to show us where we had already been. Think "Hansel and Gretel" meets "Maze Mania." To our dismay, we looked down to find that there were thousands of tiny shreds of paper at our feet, left by others who had tried the same thing.

In the midst of our chaos and confusion, we looked up and saw people watching us from a porch above the maze. We implored them to help us, and with their assistance we finally made it out of the gigantic maze: not in four minutes, but in fifty-five.

Later, I realized that our lives are a lot like that maze. Just as the maze operators could change or move the doors as they saw fit, God can see the big picture and is directing us where to go by opening and closing the doors in front of us. The big difference is that while human operators might work against us, God is always directing us toward the ultimate prize. Occasionally, it may seem as though he has put obstacles in our way to make things harder for us. Yet in actuality, we cannot see or know what he has protected us from.

In the maze, I had to make decisions about which way I thought was best. If I chose incorrectly, I would encounter a closed door. So in life God directs us through opened and closed doors. When God says yes or no to your prayers by opening or closing doors, realize that he is compassionately directing your steps. He alone knows what is best for you. Just remember to look up for direction.

And stay away from mazes at the beach.

Prayer Starters

What is the most frustrating thing about the decision you have to make right now?

_____

_____

_____

_____

What godly people has the Lord put into your life to give you good advice?

_____

_____

_____

_____

Do you see any open or closed doors in your path yet? What are they?

_____

_____

_____

_____

_____

Scripture Assignment
Proverbs 3:5-6

A Prayer for When You Have to Make a Decision

Dear all-knowing God,

I am faced with a tough decision right now. The effects of my decision will be far-reaching. I know I have to make the decision but I am so afraid of making the wrong choice. Though I can take a few different paths, I am paralyzed in my indecision. I pray that you will show me the decision you would have me make. Allow me to recognize your leading.

I ask all these things in your name,

Amen

FOURTEEN

When You Struggle With Your Quiet Time

Jacob came to know the Lord at a young age, in a children's class at his church. As Jacob grew up he saw the need for his own daily quiet time. He started by working through a devotional book that assigned him a certain Scripture every day and gave him room to journal his thoughts about the verses. Soon, Jacob was in the youth group with other teens who were doing devotions. He found it encouraging to be in a group of peers who also spent time with God.

Yet in Jacob's final year in the youth group, his parents went through a very difficult separation. Jacob didn't quite know how to handle it. The first thing that changed in his life was his time with God. Jacob was angry, so he avoided his time with God. The more Jacob skipped his quiet time, the harder it was to begin again. It became easier for him to skip youth group as well. He already felt far from God and didn't want to deal with his problems.

Eight years later, Jacob has still not regained a consistent walk with God. He has faced many trials and heartaches. Some of those could have been avoided or made easier if he had continued to let God teach him.

We can let the small things in our lives slip very easily, but some "small" things have large consequences. A daily quiet time is one of those little things that is easy to forget or ignore, but the price we must pay for our separation from God is not a small one.

151

What Is a Quiet Time?

A quiet time is a specific time that most Christians set aside to spend talking to and listening to God. A quiet time usually includes Bible study, personal worship of God, and prayer. Charles Stanley, in his *Handbook for Christian Living*, explains that, "A quiet time is a basic ingredient in a maturing relationship with God. Time alone with God moves our experience as believers out of the realm of religion and into the realm of relationship."[1]

Isn't that what we all want? Not just religion but a *real* relationship with God? A daily quiet time can help us get there. It's what separates the men from the boys, so to speak. Those who are serious about God and about serving him see a quiet time as an essential activity.

A quiet time is also very personal. Everyone must come up with his or her own individual recipe for a successful quiet time. My friend Leslie prays early in the morning as she takes a walk around her neighborhood. She feels that this kind of quiet time gives her a good start in the morning and provides exercise. Another friend of mine, Daniel, prays every morning in his car on the way to work and reads the scriptures before he goes to bed that night. Everyone has his or her own way of quietly being with the Lord.

Listen to the psalmist describe his quiet time experience.

Come and listen, all you who fear God; let me tell you what he has done for me. I cried out to him with my mouth; his praise was on my tongue. If I had cherished sin in my heart, the Lord would not have listened; but

God has surely listened and heard my voice in prayer. Praise be to God, who has not rejected my prayer or withheld his love from me!

PSALM 66:16-20

Notice the three parts of a quiet time that the psalmist mentions in these verses. First, before he asked for anything in prayer, "praise was on [his] tongue." Praising God is simply taking time to thank God for who he is and what he has done for us. We can also do this by singing our praises to God. Next the psalmist refers to confession, "If I had cherished sin in my heart, the Lord would not have listened." Confession is when we look at our hearts to see if there are any sins for which we need to ask forgiveness. Once we are forgiven we can come into God's presence with our requests, which is the third and final part of our quiet time.

Why Is a Quiet Time So Important?

I am not an avid gardener and I didn't enjoy biology, but I do know a few basic things about growing plants. A plant requires water and sunlight, which provide vitamins for it to grow. When we take care of a plant we don't water it and then plant it outside in the middle of the winter. It wouldn't survive long at all! It must be strengthened and nurtured. The nutrients it receives from the soil, water, and sunlight protect it, strengthen it, and help it grow.

A quiet time is our time to receive protection from temptation, be strengthened by the Lord for our daily battles, and learn the lessons we need to grow and produce fruit (or results) in our lives. In the book *A Handbook for Christian Maturity*, Campus Crusade founder Bill Bright explains the importance of a quiet time: "The study of the Word of God and the practice of prayer are vitally important for spiritual growth. We may miss a day without feeding on the Word of God or praying and not feel any apparent ill effects in our lives, but if we continue this practice, we will lose the power to live the victorious Christian life."[2]

One of my greatest spiritual battles is controlling my tongue, and I have personally experienced the connection between missed quiet times and days that I lost this battle. In the South, to say something unkind is to say something "ugly." I remember several times in high school when "ugly" words came from my mouth. Most of the times when that happened, I had missed my quiet time the night before. I had missed the opportunity to ask God to set a guard before my mouth so that my words would please him. The days I chose to skip my quiet times were the days when I chose to enter into the world without protection, strength, and the opportunity to grow in the Lord. Again, in his *Handbook for Christian Living*, Charles Stanley captures this thought: "A person with no devotional life generally struggles with faith and obedience. After all, it is difficult to trust someone you don't know, and it is difficult to obey someone you don't trust."[3]

Our faith and our obedience are weakened when we do not spend time with God. A quiet time is like an athlete's time in the gym. In order to perform well on the field, an athlete must take time to train every day. He must increase his strength, his endurance, and his skill in order to get off the bench.

Quiet times are our training sessions with the Lord, our time to spend alone with the Coach. Usually a coach must focus on spending time with the whole team. He or she rarely has time to spend with a player one on one. Isn't it amazing that although God has billions of children, and countless other things to focus on, he desires to spend time alone with us every day? Can you imagine a whole team of players who spent time with their coach one on one every day? I think they would be unstoppable!

As Christians, we are all players on God's team, but only those players who take time to train and grow will have success in the game. Just like there are specific positions that each of the players hold, there are specific jobs that God has designed for each of us to accomplish. During our lives, God will call us into the game. Will we be ready?

Why Is It So Hard to Stick With It?

Everyone who has tried knows that it's hard to regularly keep a quiet time. The simple reason is that we are busy! A teen-ager's life is one of constant activity and constant noise. The noises of your friends' voices, your CD player, and that annoying sound that announces an instant message on the computer are always going to be louder than the quiet voice of the Lord, calling you to spend time with him. However, the more time you spend with God, the more you will be in tune with his voice.

The time you choose for your quiet time could also be a help or a hindrance to your devotions. There is no "right" time of the day for your quiet time. Some people are morning people and some are not. I have my devotions right before I go to bed, because I like going to sleep with the peaceful feeling that I am falling asleep in his hands. The downside is that this comes with the temptation to simply fall asleep. Others find that the morning works best for them and helps set a good tone for the day.

To find your own recipe, try different times and places, then record the benefits and drawbacks of each. Once you find a time that works well for you, schedule that time for God. Make an appointment with God every day. Put it on your calendar or day planner, if you use one. If we don't have a specific time to meet with God, it often won't happen.

Sometimes the method by which we choose to do our devotions is a hindrance. Different people prefer different methods. A few of my friends like to pray out loud or in their minds, while others like to write down their prayers. Some journal them by hand and others put them on the computer.

There are thousands of different methods and versions of quiet times. Some people read a psalm every night along with a few verses of another book they are working through. Some people work from devotional books; some use a program that allows them to read through the Bible in a year. There are plenty of ways to do your own devotions. I would suggest that you explore and decide what works for you and create your own personal way of observing a quiet time.

Having a quiet time every day with the Lord is sometimes difficult, because it forces us to deal with our problems. Although dealing with and working through our problems is the healthy thing to do, sometimes we don't want to face things.

When my grandmother died, one of the hardest things for me to do was to spend a lot of time talking to God. I did pray. (I wouldn't have made it without prayer.) However, I did not want to tell God how I was feeling and what I was going through. It felt to me that if I dealt with my pain before God, I was admitting that she was really gone. I know it does not make much sense logically. Yet when you go through something that is extremely difficult, it is often hard to admit that it has really happened.

It took a while before I was able to express to God all that was going on in my heart and mind. Still, I am glad I finally did. If my friend Jacob had dealt with his pain before God when his parents separated, he probably would still be close to God now. Allowing our devotions to slip is the first step down a path away from God.

Like everything else, we won't always succeed. It is very disappointing to try and try to be consistent in your time with God but still fail. However, don't let this slow you down or stop you. Each time you fall, you have a chance to renew your vigor and commit again to serving him faithfully. Even if you find a new method for your quiet time, you may still slip up again. The important thing to realize is that you must keep getting up.

Struggling with our quiet time is a problem that all Christians face at one time or another. Learning to be consistent and making the most of our devotions are two of the hardest lessons in the Christian walk. Sometimes we expect to be spiritual superheroes who never stumble or fall, but we are human. Most importantly, God knows we are human, and he is there to pick us up and cheer us on every step of the way. "I will instruct thee and teach thee in the way which thou shalt go: I will guide thee with mine eye" (Ps 32:8, KJV).

Prayer Starters

How do you feel when you miss your quiet time?

_____

_____

_____

How does missing your quiet time negatively affect your life?

_____

_____

_____

What are some of the reasons you have been struggling with your quiet time?

_____

_____

_____

_____

What are some other times or methods that you might try that could help you in your quiet time?

_____

_____

_____

_____

Scripture Assignment
1 John 5:14-15; 2 Chronicles 7:14

A Prayer for When You Struggle With Your Quiet Time

Dear heavenly Father,

It seems that no matter how hard I try, I keep missing quiet times. I am sorry for my inconsistency. I know that I will not grow into the Christian you would like me to be unless I spend time with you. Life just gets so busy sometimes. I know that isn't an excuse. Please forgive me, and help me to set aside a time each day to spend with you. Thank you for never forgetting me!

In your mercy,

Amen

FIFTEEN

When You Have Been Mistreated

Tracey and Mark had just broken up after dating quite seriously for most of their junior and senior years of high school. They knew that above all they wanted to remain friends.

In the last semester of their senior year, a new boy named Andy transferred in to their high school. The new guy intrigued Tracey, perhaps only because he was new. Gradually Tracey and Andy grew closer and closer. Andy listened to Tracey talk about Mark and all their misunderstandings and problems. He comforted and encouraged her like no one else could. Andy realized that Tracey still cared about Mark and knew that if he ever wanted a shot at dating Tracey, he needed to create some space between these two friendly ex's.

Mark, on the other hand, simply wanted the best for Tracey. It hurt him sometimes to see that Tracey had replaced him with Andy so quickly, but he wanted only the best for her. A basketball player for the school, Mark often hung around after the games to talk and laugh with his friends. One day he noticed that there was a newcomer to this after-game ritual: Andy. Mark approached Andy first and extended his hand. Andy smiled and shook his hand. They made some small talk before Andy invited Mark out to get a hamburger with him. Mark thought this was a bit strange, but he thought that he should get to know Andy since Tracey was so close to him.

Oddly enough, Mark and Andy got along quite well. They

laughed and joked and enjoyed the night. By the time they had each finished up a chocolate sundae it was time for the real business of the night.

Mark put his spoon down on the table, took a deep breath, and said, "Andy, I want you to know that I care about Tracey and want the best for her, and if you ever want to date her, go right ahead." Tears began to form in his eyes. "I only want her to be happy."

"Thank you. I know you truly mean that," answered Andy. They paid the check and went their separate ways.

The next week at school, Mark felt great about life. He had made peace with Tracey's new man and he had expressed his desire for friendship with Tracey. He had settled his emotional business. During lunch, he happened to get in line right behind Tracey.

"Hey, Tracey."

She did not answer. She just shrugged her shoulders and left the line. Mark could not figure out what was going on. Later that day, he took one of Tracey's friends aside and asked what was going on. To Mark's shock, he learned that Andy had gone back to Tracey and told her all about the dinner he had had with Mark. However, Andy had decided to make up his own version of the conversation. Andy had told Tracey that Mark was crying uncontrollably at dinner about how much he needed to have her back in his life. Andy had managed to make Mark look like a psycho-ex. Tracey did not want to make the situation worse, so she had decided to give up on the friendship between them.

Tracey and Mark never regained their friendship. Mark had done everything right, only to have everything go wrong.

That's Not Fair

One of the biggest shocks I had as a child was learning that life was unfair. I learned this lesson when a teacher's daughter, who was in my second-grade class, pushed me down on the playground. Normally, it wouldn't have been a big deal, but I broke my finger when I fell. Every other student who had pushed another was punished, but not the teacher's daughter. Yep, life isn't always fair. Things that should happen sometimes do not; things that should not happen sometimes do.

I do not think that we are any less shocked by this truth when we get older. When unfairness occurs, we feel cheated, robbed, disrespected, hurt, swindled, and forgotten. Our jaws drop to the ground and we cannot understand why we have been mistreated.

Dealing With Your Mistreatment

If I were to throw a tennis ball at a brick wall, I would expect it to suddenly bounce back at me. The reaction of the ball does not surprise me. Imagine now that I am just walking down a street when a tennis ball comes flying out of nowhere and nails me in the head. That is what it feels like to be mistreated. We do not understand why it happens. We have done nothing to cause the pain we have received.

I lived in West Virginia when I was very young. My father's church was in a rural area in a small town. We did not receive cable TV or even all of the local channels. I grew up without "Sesame Street" or "Mr. Rogers." My grandparents used to record "Tom and Jerry" off of their TV and send me the videotapes. Some of my favorite episodes involved a large bulldog who came to Jerry's aid. For those of you from the "Animaniac" generation who are not familiar with this cartoon, Tom was a cat and Jerry the mouse he chased. Whenever Tom would try to pull a trick on Jerry, Jerry would run to the bulldog, who would then punch Tom's lights out. Sometimes, Jerry would even 'sic' the bulldog on Tom for no reason at all.

When we are wronged, our first response often is to find a way to get back at the person who hurt us. We don't even have to think about whether we want to do this. Revenge is a desire that comes quite naturally, which is exactly why we should not give in to it. Remember, the easiest thing to do is rarely the right thing to do. Although we want to find a bulldog and set him loose on the person who has mistreated us, that is just the opposite of what God wants us to do.

The horrible things Christ had to go through to obtain our salvation are the ultimate example of mistreatment. Nothing he went through was deserved. Yet, Peter wrote, "When they hurled their insults at him, he did not retaliate; when he suffered, he made no threats. Instead, he entrusted himself to him who judges justly" (1 Pt 2:23). He endured and left the revenge part up to God, to do or not to do.

The best thing to remember when you are mistreated is to embrace God. Even if you could find a bulldog to make your revenge, you wouldn't really feel better afterward. Probably you'd only feel worse, because you would have stooped to the other person's level. Only prayer and the peace that the Holy Spirit brings will salve your hurt. God is still in control and will carry you through to the other side of your pain.

When I was fifteen, our church started a second worship service at 8:45 A.M. I had already started "subbing" for other teachers of children's classes, but I was eager to do more. I wanted to have a class of my own. I decided that since no one was willing to teach the few children who attended the early service, I would.

I started reading book after book about teaching, about children, and about teaching children. I approached my father about the idea of an early service kids' class, since he was the senior pastor at the church. He loved the idea but said that it was up to the youth pastor. Pastor Jack was a charismatic guy that every teen liked. He was an entertaining Bible teacher and fun to be around. I approached him with the idea of teaching the kids as soon as I could. I was so excited. I had already planned some lessons and chosen some crafts. I explained my heart's desire to Pastor Jack, hoping he would understand. When I was finished, he leaned way back in his black office chair, and said, "I don't think so."

I felt bullied or betrayed, I wasn't sure which. I could understand him choosing someone else over me. After all, I was only fifteen and I'd never had my own class before. Yet he wasn't choosing someone over me; he was choosing to not have *anyone* teach the kids instead of letting me teach. Taking my father's advice, I waited patiently, hoping he would change his mind.

I waited for several months before I was finally allowed to teach. When the time came, it was right. God gave me the privilege of leading sixteen children to the Lord in the two and a half years I taught the class. The experience I received from teaching those classes has changed my life. Sometimes it feels like we are being mistreated, but God knows the right time for us to serve him. The Lord will eventually exalt those who remain faithful. Entrust yourself to him who judges justly.

The Reality of Persecution

Persecution is a severe form of mistreatment that comes to God's people because of their beliefs. The reason behind this type of suffering is very clear, but with that clarity comes a heavy burden.

Persecution is a bigger problem than most of us realize. According to the book *Jesus Freaks*, there were 165,000 martyrs in the year 2000.[1] The book is filled with story after story about young martyrs from around the world. In some religions, if you convert to Christianity, your own family will kill you. Most of us assume that full-blown persecution will never touch our lives, but we are wrong.

If we are committed Christians we will be persecuted in some way for our faith, even if our lives are not physically threatened. Speaking out against homosexuality or abortion is becoming dangerous in today's society. Speaking out for prayer in schools, abstinence programs, or basic Christian beliefs can also be threatening. Should that opposition and possible danger prevent us from speaking out? Never.

Jesus Freaks, compiled with help from The Voice of the Martyrs, records a true story of a sixteen-year-old girl from Asia who loved her Lord too much to give in to threats of persecution.

The Communist soldiers had discovered their illegal Bible study. "We will let you go," he growled, "but first you must spit on this book of lies. Anyone who refuses will be shot." The believers had no choice but to obey the officer's orders.

A soldier pointed his gun at one of the men. "You first." The man slowly got up and knelt down by the Bible. Reluctantly he spit on it, praying, "Father please forgive me."

Others followed, but then it was the girl's turn.

Quietly, she came forward. Overcome with love for her Lord, she knelt down and picked up the Bible. She wiped off the spit with her dress. "What have they done to Your Word? Please forgive them," she prayed. The Communist soldier put his pistol to her head. Then he pulled the trigger.[2]

The Challenge of Mistreatment

The apostle Paul was beaten and thrown in jail several times for teaching the gospel. He eventually died a martyr's death. Listen to his words:

> You, however, know all about my teaching, my way of life, my purpose, faith, patience, love, endurance, persecutions, sufferings—what kinds of things happened to me in Antioch, Iconium and Lystra, the persecutions I endured. Yet the Lord rescued me from all of them. In fact, everyone who wants to live a godly life in Christ Jesus will be

persecuted, while evil men and impostors will go from bad to worse, deceiving and being deceived. But as for you, continue in what you have learned and have become convinced of, because you know those from whom you learned it.

2 TIMOTHY 3:10-14

Paul is saying that when we serve the Lord, he will be faithful to rescue us from our persecutions. Sometimes he does not protect us from all of the physical persecution. Yet he will always be there to give us the ultimate victory through eternal life in Christ.

Moving Past Our Mistreatment

Whenever I think of moving past something, the phrase "forgive and forget" comes to my mind. But, hey, let's face it. You and I most likely will not forget the bad things that have happened to us. Still, it is possible to forgive the person or persons who have wronged us.

Not only is it possible for us, however, but the Bible commands us to forgive. "Bless those who persecute you; bless and do not curse" (Rom 12:14). It isn't a matter of not taking revenge; it is a matter of going to the other extreme and showing *love* toward those who hurt us.

All I can say is praise the Lord that we have the Spirit of God to help us out, because we could *not* do this alone!

Prayer Starters

How have you been been mistreated, and how does this make you feel?

_____

_____

_____

_____

_____

What things can you do to help you forgive the person or persons who mistreated you?

_____

_____

_____

_____

_____

_____

How did this mistreatment affect you, and what did you learn from the experience?

_____

_____

_____

_____

_____

Scripture Assignment
Matthew 5:10-12

A Prayer for When You Have Been Mistreated

Father,

I don't understand why there are people in this world that would hurt me for their own gain. I did not deserve this, but I know that your Son did not deserve mistreatment, either. Help me to accept your sovereignty in my life and forgive those who have hurt me. I do not want to hold on to bitterness or resentment.

Help me to forgive in this unfair world,

Amen

SIXTEEN

When Life Doesn't Make Sense

Employees went to work, students went to school, and children went out to play on September 11, 2001. America was comfortable, but September 11 was not a regular day. None of us could have known the terrible events that would unfold.

On that seemingly ordinary morning, members of al-Qaida, a terrorist group led by Muslim extremist Osama bin Laden, struck America with a series of violent attacks. American Airlines Flight 11, en route from Boston to Los Angeles, was hijacked and flown into the north tower of the World Trade Center in New York City at 8:45 A.M. Eighteen minutes later, United Airlines Flight 175 crashed into the World Trade Center's south tower. Thousands of people were still trying to escape as the burning towers collapsed onto the streets.

The terror was not focused solely on Manhattan. Less than an hour after the first tower was hit, American Airlines Flight 77 crashed into the Pentagon, causing nearly two hundred deaths and many more casualties. The final blow came when a second United Airlines flight went down in Somerset County, Pennsylvania, apparently piloted into the ground by passengers determined to stop the hijackers from using the plane as a weapon of mass destruction.

Countless lives were touched by this act of war waged against the United States. The country was gripped by fear and sorrow as we watched the towers fall and the Pentagon burn. None of us had thought that something of this magnitude could take place on *our* soil with *our* planes.

Yet life doesn't always make sense, and God doesn't always give us the answers. It is during these times of total uncertainty that we can be most tempted to mistrust God. After these terrorist attacks, there was one question on many people's minds: "Why would God allow this to happen?"

"Why, God, Why?"

In the wake of 9-11, church pews around the world overflowed with churchgoers. George Barna, director of Barna Research, said, "after the attack, millions of nominally churched or generally irreligious Americans were desperately seeking something that would restore stability and a sense of meaning to life."[1] While conducting research on church attendance after 9-11, Barna found that church attendance initially exploded, only to dwindle away in the weeks and months following the national crisis. Why did this occur? Barna suggests that the local churches failed to properly meet the needs of the new crowds. "Our assessment is that churches succeeded at putting on a friendly face but failed at motivating the vast majority of spiritual explorers to connect with Christ in a more intimate or intense manner."[2]

I believe Barna's assessment to be true, but I also believe there was a bigger reason why people left the churches. I think people went to church looking for reasons for the tragedy and answers to their questions about it, not looking for God. When Christian leaders could not produce exact reasons for what happened or solutions for their pain, people went away, discouraged and disillusioned. This seems tragic to me, because although God sometimes lets us in on some of his reasons for allowing things or doing things, most of the time he doesn't. "'For my thoughts are not your thoughts, neither are your ways my ways,' declares the Lord. 'As the heavens are higher than the earth, so are my ways higher than your ways and my thoughts than your thoughts'" (Is 55:8-9).

We must realize that we are the created beings and God is the Creator. How *could* we understand his reasoning? Dr. James Dobson shares, in *Life on the Edge*: "Clearly Scripture tells us we lack the capacity to grasp God's infinite mind or the way He intervenes in our lives. How arrogant of us to think otherwise. Trying to analyze His omnipotence is like an amoeba attempting to comprehend the behavior of man."[3]

When disasters strike, we feel like children at God's feet, tugging at his coat with the question, "Why?" It is human nature for us to want to understand each significant event in our lives. When my grandmother died, I wanted to know why. When a car hit my neighbor's dog, she wanted to know why. We feel that if we could just grab hold of a reason for each painful event then we could make it through to the other side. This pull-yourself-up-by-your-bootstraps mentality has one major flaw: If we always have a reason for things, we will be tempted to rely on ourselves during our pain rather than turning to God. We are not meant to understand; we are meant to trust.

God's reasons are beyond our created minds. He does not promise us any explanations on earth, but one day in heaven we will understand our pain. "Now I know in part; then I shall know fully, even as I am fully known" (1 Cor 13:12).

How to Respond When Life Doesn't Make Sense

As with every disappointment, we have a decision to make when trouble or disaster strikes. How will we respond? The first part of responding correctly when life doesn't make sense is keeping our focus on God.

One morning, on what I thought to be a typical Sunday, I woke up, got dressed, grabbed my Sunday school lesson, and rushed out the door. As I charged out of the heavy outer doors to my dorm, I noticed that four inches of snow had fallen the night before. No big deal. The state of Ohio always keeps the roads clear, and I saw several other cars braving the weather as other drivers made their way to church.

I started my car and backed out of the parking space with a slight slide of my wheels. Nonetheless, I turned onto the main road with confidence. As I came upon a curve in the road, I noticed a car had just gone into a ditch. As I slowed down so as not to hit the various people and cars, I hit the same slick spot the other car had. I found my little North Carolina self behind the wheel of an out-of-control SUV on Ohio snow and ice.

The brakes were of no use. I was totally helpless. I soon realized that I was sliding quickly toward the other car. I had to do something. I somehow managed to steer my car away from the people and cars, into a large green road sign. (I think my guardian angel was pushing my car from the back.) My car did suffer some damage, but not nearly as much as it would have if I had crashed anywhere else. (The road sign wasn't as lucky.)

At some point in our lives, we will all spin out of control. We won't know how and we won't know why. How we attempt to steer our out-of-control lives, however, is up to us. We can choose to focus on exactly why God has allowed this situation and how it came about, or we can focus on trusting God for the next step.

In addition to keeping our focus on God, it is important to remember his infinite love for us. The presence of pain and disappointment in our lives does not mean that he does not love us. It actually means that he loves us all the more.

> In this you greatly rejoice, though now for a little while you may have had to suffer grief in all kinds of trials. These have come so that your faith—of greater worth than gold, which perishes even though refined by fire—may be proved genuine and may result in praise, glory, and honor when Jesus Christ is revealed.
>
> 1 PETER 1:6-7

He loves us more than we could ever comprehend, and because he loves us, he knows the people and things that are precious to us. Michelle McKinney Hammond describes his care for our concerns:

> Just as single women can believe in God for everything except a mate and mothers can believe God for everything except their children, the same principle prevails here. We have trouble releasing our most precious things into the care of God. For some reason, we do not believe that what we view as precious is even more precious to God and that He is well able to keep those things we hold dear. How it wrenches our hearts when we have done

everything we can think of, yet to no avail, and we are forced to release our dreams, our mates, and our children into the hands of God, stand still, and see His salvation.[4]

If God loves us as much as he promises in his Word (see Jn 3:16), then he also is capable of taking care of those things we hold dear. When life doesn't make sense we should focus on God, remember his love, and finally take the next step in our growth.

There are lessons that we must learn through painful circumstances that we could learn only by going through them. Remember the story of Job? He lost his family, his wealth, his health, and his friends but grew closer to God. Ultimately, for Job's faithfulness the Lord blessed him with a larger family and more wealth than he'd had before. We must look for the lessons that God has in store for us during our trying times. It is all part of growing.

Michelle McKinney Hammond explains in *Prayer Guide for the Brokenhearted:* "Yes, he leads us. Sometimes forward, sometimes back. Forward to new pastures. Changing our diet from the familiar 'comfort food' to richer bread, heartier meat. Nourishment to make the blood thicker, to add marrow to the bones and flesh to the body."[5]

A Sovereign Bullet

Jim and Veronica "Roni" Bowers had committed their lives to mission work. While on the mission field in Peru in April

2001, their small plane was mistaken for a drug-running aircraft and shot down by a Peruvian air force fighter. Their small Cessna floatplane crashed into the Amazon River, but Roni and the Bowers' seven-month-old daughter, Charity, were already dead—killed by bullets that had struck the small craft. Jim, his six-year-old son, and the pilot survived and were rescued in canoes.

Pastor Bill Rudd of Calvary Church in Fruitport, Michigan—home church for the Bowers family—spoke at Cedarville University earlier this year. Pastor Rudd talked with us about Jim Bowers' extraordinary forgiveness of the Peruvian pilots, saying that at the funeral for his wife and daughter, Jim Bowers spoke publicly about his forgiveness and also told the crowd that he believed that the bullet that killed his wife and daughter was a "sovereign bullet."

That phrase stuck out to me as I realized the extreme faith of this missionary. He recognized that God had allowed that bullet to take his wife's and daughter's lives. He knew that God is in control of this universe, period. Jim Bowers did not question why this tragedy wasn't miraculously prevented; he simply focused on God, remembered his love, and took the next step in his growth, which for him was to forgive the pilots.

Trust Is "A Must"

As children of God, it is crucial for us to trust God and all his ways. If we don't want to be driven crazy by the question of "Why?" we must realize that sometimes there are no answers. Dr. James Dobson shares from his book, *When God Doesn't*

Make Sense: "If we truly understood the majesty of the Lord and the depth of His love for us, we would certainly accept those times when He defies human logic and sensibilities. Indeed, that is what we *must* do."[6]

Though this kind of trust is against our nature and contrary to our logic, it is our only choice if we are to truly rest in God.

Prayer Starters

Why is it difficult for you to trust God when life doesn't make sense?

_____

_____

_____

_____

How does it make you feel to not understand the pain you are going through?

_____

_____

_____

_____

What are some lessons that God might be teaching you in your pain?

_____

_____

_____

_____

Scripture Assignment
Isaiah 41:10

A Prayer for When Life Doesn't Make Sense

Dear all-knowing, all-loving Father,

I am facing one of the hardest battles of my faith. You don't make sense to me right now, Father. I don't understand why things happen that you could prevent. My mind and my heart cry out for reasons and answers, yet I know that may not be for me to know right now. Everyone around me thinks I am crazy to remain faithful to you, but I know that it is my only choice. Either you are God in control of the universe or you are not God at all. I believe that you love me and want what is best for me, even when it doesn't feel that way. Give me strength and grace to fight this battle. Help me to focus on you, remember your love, and take the next step.

In your almighty name,

Amen

Conclusion

At some point, we have all been mad, sad, or just totally confused.

No matter what your circumstance—whether a crushing crush or overwhelming despair, stress, or fear, any of the other issues we talked about in this book, or one we didn't yet touch upon—you may have heard someone say, "You don't have a prayer." Perhaps you've said this to yourself. What is meant is that you don't have a chance of making it through your situation healthy and whole and able to enjoy life. I am here to assure you that you do.

I have experienced or been touched by all of the emotions and heartaches discussed in this book. Life was difficult at times, but I knew that my hope, "my prayer," was in God. There *is* hope in times of darkness. When you and I are mad, sad, totally confused, or hurting or struggling in any other way, God wants us to turn to him: "That we through patience and comfort of the Scriptures might have hope" (Rom 15:4, KJV).

No matter what you face today or what you face in the future, remember that God is bigger than your mistakes, bigger than your pain, and bigger than your enemies. He is your loving Father, just waiting to wipe away your tears.

May all your prayers be glorifying as you live each day in his light.

Recommended Reading

The 7 Habits of Highly Effective Teens
by Sean Covey
Simon & Schuster

Don't Sweat the Small Stuff for Teens
by Richard Carlson, Ph.D.
Hyperion

10 Challenges of a WorldChanger
by Ron Luce
Thomas Nelson

Life on the Edge
by Dr. James Dobson
W Publishing Group

Prayer Guide for the Brokenhearted
by Michelle McKinney Hammond
Servant Publications

God Thinks You're Positively Awesome!
by Andrea Stephens
Servant Publications

Get a Love Life
by Michelle McKinney Hammond
Harvest House Publishers

A Ready Defense
by Josh McDowell
Nelson Reference

Notes

ONE
When You Are Stressed Out

1. Jeff Davidson, *The Complete Idiot's Guide to Managing Stress* (New York: Alpha, 1997), 17.
2. Davidson, 17.
3. Dr. Thomas Whiteman, Dr. Sam Verghese, Randy Petersen, *The Complete Stress Management Workbook* (Grand Rapids, Mich.: Zondervan, 1996), 232.
4. Jeff Cohen, "Worried About Your Health in College?" Medscape Health for Consumers, www.health.medscape.com, April 2000.
5. Ben Ferguson, *God, I've Got a Problem* (Santa Ana, Calif.: Vision House, 1974), 67.

TWO
When You Are Struggling With Your Self-Image

1. Charles Stanley, *Our Unmet Needs* (Nashville, Tenn.: Thomas Nelson, 1999), 226.
2. Andrea Stephens, *God Thinks You're Positively Awesome!* (Ann Arbor, Mich.: Servant, 1997), 21.

THREE
When You Are Afraid

1. Kent Crockett, *The 911 Handbook: Biblical Solutions to Everyday Problems* (Peabody, Mass.: Hendrickson, 1997), 119.

FOUR
When Everything Goes Wrong

1. Crockett, 168.

FIVE
When You Feel Like a Failure

1. John C. Maxwell, *Failing Forward* (Nashville, Tenn.: Thomas Nelson, 2000), 27-30.
2. Robert Schuller, *Tough Times Never Last, But Tough People Do* (Nashville, Tenn.: Bantam, by arrangement with Thomas Nelson, 1984), 202.

SIX
When Divorce Hits

1. Debbie Barr, "Helping Children of Divorce," *Discipleship Journal*, May-June 1993, 53.
2. Carolyn Johnson, *How to Blend a Family* (Grand Rapids, Mich.: Zondervan, 1989), 36.

SEVEN
When You Lose a Loved One

1. Zig Ziglar, *Confessions of a Grieving Christian* (Nashville, Tenn.: Thomas Nelson, 1998), 270.
2. Erwin Lutzer, *Managing Your Emotions* (Wheaton, Ill.: Victor, 1983), 146.

EIGHT
When You Have Unsaved Loved Ones

1. Darrell W. Robinson, *People Sharing Jesus* (Nashville, Tenn.: Thomas Nelson, 1995), 67.

NINE
When You Are Sick of Being Single

1. *Webster's Dictionary for Everyday Use* (Baltimore, Md.: Ottenheimer, 1958), 348.
2. *Webster's Dictionary for Everyday Use*, 348.
3. Richard Carlson, *Don't Sweat the Small Stuff for Teens* (New York: Hyperion, 2000), 122.
4. George Bernard Shaw, "Saint Joan," scene 5, in *Seven Plays* (New York: Dodd, Mead & Company, 1959), 864.

TEN
When You Are Crushed by a Crush

1. Carlson, 237.

ELEVEN
When You Go Through a Breakup

1. Dick Innes, *How to Mend a Broken Heart* (Grand Rapids, Mich.: Baker Book House, 1994), 31.
2. Innes, 43.

TWELVE
When You've Made a Mistake

1. Lutzer, 119.

FOURTEEN
When You Struggle With Your Quiet Time

1. Charles Stanley, *Charles Stanley's Handbook for Christian Living* (Nashville, Tenn.: Thomas Nelson, 2000), 501.
2. Bill Bright, A *Handbook for Christian Maturity* (Orlando, Fla.: New Life, 1994), 179.
3. Stanley, 501.

FIFTEEN
When You Have Been Mistreated

1. *Jesus Freaks* (Tulsa, Okla.: Albury, 1999), 15.
2. *Jesus Freaks,* 51.

SIXTEEN
When Life Doesn't Make Sense

1. www.barna.org.
2. www.barna.org.
3. James Dobson, *Life on the Edge* (Dallas, Tex.: W Publishing Group, 1995), 247-48.
4. Michelle McKinney Hammond, *The Power of Femininity* (Eugene, Ore.: Harvest House, 1999), 170.
5. Michelle McKinney Hammond, *Prayer Guide for the Brokenhearted* (Ann Arbor, Mich.: Servant, 2000), 38.
6. James Dobson, *When God Doesn't Make Sense* (Wheaton, Ill.: Tyndale House, 1993), 69.